Favorite Brand Name™

BEST-LOVED

Pumpkin, Sweet Potato, & Squash Recipes

Publications International, Ltd.

Pictured on the front cover *(left to right):* Sweet Potato Fries *(page 152),* Southern-Style Pumpkin Cheesecake *(page 74)* and Barley and Pear-Stuffed Acorn Squash *(page 189).*

Pictured on the back cover *(left to right):* Balsamic Butternut Squash *(page 205),* Sweet Potato Bisque *(page 118)* and Pumpkin White Chocolate Drops *(page 44).*

ISBN: 978-1-68022-444-3

Library of Congress Control Number: 2016934623

Manufactured in China.

8 7 6 5 4 3 2 1

Microwave Cooking: Microwave ovens vary in wattage. Use the cooking times as guidelines and check for doneness before adding more time.

Pumpkin
RECIPES

Pumpkin for Breakfast

Chocolate-Cranberry Pumpkin Pancakes

MAKES 16 TO 18 (4-INCH) PANCAKES

2 cups all-purpose flour

⅓ cup packed brown sugar

2 teaspoons baking powder

½ teaspoon salt

½ teaspoon ground cinnamon

¼ teaspoon baking soda

¼ teaspoon ground ginger

¼ teaspoon ground nutmeg

1½ cups milk

2 eggs

½ cup canned pumpkin

¼ cup vegetable oil

½ cup mini semisweet chocolate chips

½ cup dried cranberries

⅓ cup cinnamon chips

1 to 2 teaspoons butter, plus additional for serving

Maple syrup

1. Combine flour, brown sugar, baking powder, salt, cinnamon, baking soda, ginger and nutmeg in large bowl; mix well. Beat milk, eggs, pumpkin and oil in medium bowl until well blended. Add to flour mixture with chocolate chips, cranberries and cinnamon chips; stir just until dry ingredients are moistened.

2. Heat 1 teaspoon butter on griddle over medium heat. Pour batter by ¼ cupfuls onto griddle. Cook about 2 minutes or until bubbles form and bottom of pancakes are lightly browned. Turn and cook 2 minutes or until browned and cooked through. Repeat with remaining batter, adding remaining butter to griddle if necessary. Serve with maple syrup and additional butter, if desired.

Baked Pumpkin French Toast

MAKES 6 SERVINGS

1 tablespoon butter, softened

1 loaf challah or egg bread
(12 to 16 ounces), cut into
¾-inch-thick slices

7 eggs

1¼ cups whole milk

⅔ cup canned pumpkin

1 teaspoon vanilla

½ teaspoon pumpkin pie spice

⅛ teaspoon salt

3 tablespoons sugar

2 teaspoons ground cinnamon

Maple syrup

1. Generously grease 13×9-inch baking dish with butter. Arrange bread slices in dish, fitting slices in tightly.

2. Whisk eggs, milk, pumpkin, vanilla, pumpkin pie spice and salt in medium bowl until well blended. Pour over bread in prepared baking dish; turn slices to coat completely with egg mixture. Cover and refrigerate 8 hours or overnight.

3. Preheat oven to 350°F. Combine sugar and cinnamon in small bowl; mix well. Turn bread slices again; sprinkle generously with cinnamon-sugar.

4. Bake about 30 minutes or until bread is puffy and golden brown. Serve immediately with maple syrup.

Pumpkin Spice Mini Doughnuts

MAKES 36 DOUGHNUTS

1 tablespoon granulated sugar

2 teaspoons ground cinnamon, divided

2 cups white whole wheat flour

½ cup packed brown sugar

1½ teaspoons baking powder

½ teaspoon salt

½ teaspoon ground ginger

½ teaspoon ground nutmeg

¼ teaspoon baking soda

2 eggs

½ cup canned pumpkin

¼ cup (½ stick) butter, softened

¼ cup milk

1 teaspoon vanilla

1. Preheat oven to 350°F. Spray 36 mini (1¾-inch) muffin cups with nonstick cooking spray. Combine granulated sugar and 1 teaspoon cinnamon in shallow bowl; set aside.

2. Combine flour, brown sugar, baking powder, remaining 1 teaspoon cinnamon, salt, ginger, nutmeg and baking soda in medium bowl; mix well. Beat eggs, pumpkin, butter, milk and vanilla in large bowl with electric mixer at medium speed until well blended. Gradually add flour mixture; beat just until blended. Spoon scant tablespoonful batter into each prepared muffin cup.

3. Bake 12 minutes or until toothpick inserted into centers comes out clean. Cool in pans 2 minutes.

4. Working with one doughnut at a time, roll in cinnamon-sugar to coat. Return to wire racks to cool slightly. Serve warm or cool completely.

Pumpkin Power Smoothie

MAKES 1 SERVING

⅓ cup water

1 sweet red apple, seeded and cut into chunks

½ frozen banana

½ cup canned pumpkin

½ cup ice cubes

1 tablespoon lemon juice

1 tablespoon ground flaxseed

1 teaspoon honey

Dash ground nutmeg

Combine water, apple, banana, pumpkin, ice, lemon juice, flaxseed, honey and nutmeg in blender; blend until smooth. Serve immediately.

Spiced Pumpkin Banana Smoothie

MAKES 1 SERVING

½ cup almond milk

½ frozen banana

½ cup canned pumpkin

½ cup ice cubes

1 tablespoon honey

1 teaspoon ground flaxseed

¼ teaspoon ground cinnamon

⅛ teaspoon ground ginger

Dash ground nutmeg

Combine almond milk, banana, pumpkin, ice, honey, flaxseed, cinnamon, ginger and nutmeg in blender; blend until smooth. Serve immediately.

Pumpkin Power Smoothie

Pumpkin Waffles with Pumpkin Marmalade

MAKES 10 WAFFLES AND 4 CUPS MARMALADE

1   can (29 ounces) solid-pack pumpkin, divided

1   cup packed brown sugar

1   cup water

1   cup orange juice

1   tablespoon maple syrup

1   teaspoon finely grated orange peel

½   teaspoon ground ginger

¼   teaspoon salt

1   package (about 15 ounces) yellow cake mix

2   teaspoons pumpkin pie spice

1½   cups milk

2   eggs

¼   cup (½ stick) butter, melted

Whipped cream (optional)

1. Reserve 1 cup pumpkin; set aside for waffles. Combine remaining pumpkin, brown sugar, water, orange juice, maple syrup, orange peel, ginger and salt in medium saucepan; bring to a simmer over medium heat. Cook until mixture thickens to consistency of applesauce, stirring occasionally. Reduce heat to low; keep warm.

2. Preheat oven to 200°F. Place wire rack on baking sheet; place in oven. Preheat waffle iron according to manufacturer's directions. Spray cooking surface with nonstick cooking spray.

3. Combine cake mix and pumpkin pie spice in large bowl; mix well. Whisk milk, reserved 1 cup pumpkin, eggs and butter in medium bowl until well blended. Add to dry ingredients; stir until well blended.

4. Pour ½ cup batter into heated waffle iron. Cook until steaming stops and waffle is lightly browned and crisp. Remove to wire rack in oven to keep warm. Repeat with remaining batter. Serve with warm pumpkin marmalade and whipped cream, if desired. Refrigerate leftover marmalade.

 tip Leftover marmalade can be served on toast or with bagels and cream cheese.

Baked Pumpkin Oatmeal
MAKES 6 SERVINGS

2 cups old-fashioned oats

2 cups milk

1 cup canned pumpkin

2 eggs

⅓ cup packed brown sugar

1 teaspoon vanilla

½ cup dried cranberries, plus additional for topping

1 teaspoon pumpkin pie spice

½ teaspoon salt

½ teaspoon baking powder

Maple syrup

Chopped pecans (optional)

1. Preheat oven to 350°F. Spray 8-inch square baking dish with nonstick cooking spray.

2. Spread oats on ungreased baking sheet. Bake about 10 minutes or until fragrant and lightly browned, stirring occasionally. Pour into medium bowl; let cool slightly.

3. Whisk milk, pumpkin, eggs, brown sugar and vanilla in large bowl until well blended. Add ½ cup cranberries, pumpkin pie spice, salt and baking powder to oats; mix well. Add oat mixture to milk mixture; stir until well blended. Pour into prepared baking dish.

4. Bake about 45 minutes or until set and knife inserted into center comes out almost clean. Serve warm with maple syrup, additional cranberries and pecans, if desired.

Pumpkin Streusel Coffeecake

MAKES 9 SERVINGS

Streusel

- ½ cup all-purpose flour
- ½ cup packed brown sugar
- 2 teaspoons ground cinnamon
- ¼ cup (½ stick) butter, softened
- ½ cup chopped walnuts

Coffeecake

- 2 cups all-purpose flour
- 2 teaspoons baking powder

- ¾ teaspoon pumpkin pie spice
- ½ teaspoon baking soda
- ½ teaspoon salt
- ¾ cup packed brown sugar
- ½ cup (1 stick) butter, softened
- 2 eggs
- 1 cup canned pumpkin
- 2 teaspoons vanilla

1. Preheat oven to 325°F. Spray 8-inch square baking pan with nonstick cooking spray.

2. For streusel, combine ½ cup flour, ½ cup brown sugar and cinnamon in small bowl; mix well. Cut in ¼ cup butter with pastry blender or mix with fingers until coarse crumbs form. Stir in walnuts. Refrigerate until ready to use.

3. For coffeecake, combine 2 cups flour, baking powder, pumpkin pie spice, baking soda and salt in medium bowl. Beat ¾ cup brown sugar and ½ cup butter in large bowl with electric mixer at medium-high speed until light and fluffy. Add eggs, one at a time, beating well at medium speed after each addition. Beat in pumpkin and vanilla until well blended. Add flour mixture; beat at low speed until blended. (Batter will be very thick.) Spread half of batter in prepared baking pan; sprinkle with half of streusel. Spread remaining batter over streusel; sprinkle with remaining streusel.

4. Bake about 40 minutes or until toothpick inserted into center comes out clean. Cool completely in pan on wire rack.

Pumpkin Chocolate Chip Muffins

MAKES 18 MUFFINS

2½ cups all-purpose flour

1 tablespoon baking powder

1½ teaspoons pumpkin pie spice*

½ teaspoon salt

1 cup canned pumpkin

1 cup packed brown sugar

¾ cup milk

6 tablespoons (¾ stick) butter, melted

2 eggs

1 cup semisweet chocolate chips

½ cup chopped walnuts

*Or substitute ¾ teaspoon ground cinnamon, ½ teaspoon ground ginger and ¼ teaspoon each ground allspice and ground nutmeg.

1. Preheat oven to 400°F. Line 18 standard (2½-inch) muffin cups with paper baking cups or spray with nonstick cooking spray.

2. Combine flour, baking powder, pumpkin pie spice and salt in large bowl; mix well. Whisk pumpkin, brown sugar, milk, butter and eggs in medium bowl until well blended. Add pumpkin mixture, chocolate chips and walnuts to flour mixture; stir just until moistened. Spoon batter evenly into prepared muffin cups.

3. Bake 15 minutes or until toothpick inserted into centers comes out clean. Cool in pans 10 minutes; remove to wire racks to cool completely.

Pumpkin Granola

MAKES ABOUT 5½ CUPS

---

3 cups old-fashioned oats

¾ cup coarsely chopped almonds

¾ cup raw pumpkin seeds
   (pepitas)

½ cup canned pumpkin

½ cup maple syrup

⅓ cup coconut oil, melted

1 teaspoon vanilla

1 teaspoon ground cinnamon

½ teaspoon salt

¼ teaspoon ground ginger

¼ teaspoon ground nutmeg

   Pinch ground cloves

¾ cup dried cranberries

1. Preheat oven to 325°F. Line large rimmed baking sheet with parchment paper.

2. Combine oats, almonds and pumpkin seeds in large bowl. Whisk pumpkin, maple syrup, oil, vanilla, cinnamon, salt, ginger, nutmeg and cloves in medium bowl until well blended. Pour over oat mixture; stir until well blended and all ingredients are completely coated. Spread mixture evenly on prepared baking sheet.

3. Bake 50 to 60 minutes or until granola is golden brown and no longer moist, stirring every 20 minutes. (Granola will become more crisp as it cools.) Stir in cranberries; cool completely.

Variations For Pumpkin Chocolate Granola, follow the recipe above but reduce the amount of maple syrup to ⅓ cup and stir in ¾ cup semisweet chocolate chips after baking. You can also substitute pecans or walnuts for the almonds, and/or add ¾ cup flaked coconut to the mixture before baking.

Savory Pumpkin

Pumpkin Curry

MAKES 4 SERVINGS

1 tablespoon vegetable oil

1 package (14 ounces) extra firm tofu, drained and cut into 1-inch cubes

¼ cup Thai red curry paste

2 cloves garlic, minced

1 can (15 ounces) solid-pack pumpkin

1 can (14 ounces) coconut milk

1 cup water

1½ teaspoons salt

1 teaspoon sriracha sauce

4 cups cut-up vegetables (broccoli, cauliflower, red bell pepper, sweet potato)

½ cup peas

2 cups hot cooked rice

¼ cup chopped fresh basil (optional)

1. Heat oil in large skillet over high heat. Add tofu; cook and stir 2 to 3 minutes or until lightly browned. Add curry paste and garlic; cook and stir 1 minute or until tofu is coated. Add pumpkin, coconut milk, water, salt and sriracha; bring to a boil. Stir in vegetables.

2. Reduce heat to medium; cover and simmer 20 minutes or until vegetables are tender. Stir in peas; cook 1 minute or until heated through. Serve over rice; top with basil, if desired.

Pumpkin Mac and Cheese

MAKES 6 TO 8 SERVINGS

1 package (16 ounces) uncooked large elbow macaroni

½ cup (1 stick) butter, divided

¼ cup all-purpose flour

1½ cups milk

1 teaspoon salt, divided

¼ teaspoon ground nutmeg

⅛ teaspoon ground red pepper

2 cups (8 ounces) shredded Cheddar cheese

1 cup (4 ounces) shredded Monterey Jack cheese

1 cup canned pumpkin

1 cup panko bread crumbs

½ cup chopped hazelnuts or walnuts (optional)

⅛ teaspoon dried sage

1 cup (4 ounces) shredded Chihuahua cheese*

*If Chihuahua cheese is not available, substitute Monterey Jack cheese.

1. Preheat oven to 350°F. Spray 2-quart baking dish with nonstick cooking spray. Cook macaroni according to package directions until al dente. Drain and return to saucepan; keep warm.

2. Melt ¼ cup butter in medium saucepan over medium-high heat. Whisk in flour until smooth; cook 1 minute without browning, whisking constantly. Gradually whisk in milk in thin steady stream. Add ¾ teaspoon salt, nutmeg and red pepper; cook 2 to 3 minutes or until thickened, stirring frequently. Gradually add Cheddar and Monterey Jack, stirring after each addition until smooth. Add pumpkin; cook 1 minute or until heated through, stirring constantly. Pour sauce over pasta; stir to coat.

3. Melt remaining ¼ cup butter in small skillet over medium-low heat; cook until golden brown. Remove from heat; stir in panko, hazelnuts, if desired, sage and remaining ¼ teaspoon salt.

4. Layer half of pasta in prepared baking dish; sprinkle with ½ cup Chihuahua cheese. Top with remaining pasta; sprinkle with remaining Chihuahua cheese. Top with panko mixture.

5. Bake 25 to 30 minutes or until topping is golden brown and pasta is heated through.

Savory Pumpkin Hummus

MAKES 1½ CUPS

1 can (15 ounces) solid-pack pumpkin

3 tablespoons chopped fresh parsley, plus additional for garnish

3 tablespoons tahini

3 tablespoons fresh lemon juice

3 cloves garlic

1 teaspoon ground cumin

½ teaspoon salt

⅛ teaspoon black pepper

⅛ teaspoon ground red pepper, plus additional for garnish

Assorted vegetable sticks

1. Combine pumpkin, 3 tablespoons parsley, tahini, lemon juice, garlic, cumin, salt, black pepper and ⅛ teaspoon red pepper in food processor or blender; process until smooth. Cover and refrigerate at least 2 hours to allow flavors to develop.

2. Sprinkle with additional red pepper, if desired. Garnish with additional parsley. Serve with assorted vegetable sticks.

Pumpkin and Roasted Pepper Soup

MAKES 6 SERVINGS

2 tablespoons butter

1 red onion, chopped

1 stalk celery, chopped

3 cups chicken broth

1 can (15 ounces) solid-pack pumpkin

½ cup chopped roasted red pepper

½ teaspoon salt

½ teaspoon paprika

¼ teaspoon dried thyme

¼ teaspoon black pepper

2 tablespoons half-and-half

1. Melt butter in large saucepan over medium-high heat. Add onion and celery; cook 5 minutes or until onion is translucent, stirring occasionally.

2. Stir in broth, pumpkin, roasted red pepper, salt, paprika, thyme and black pepper; bring to a boil. Reduce heat to low; cook 30 minutes, stirring occasionally.

3. Working in batches, process soup in food processor or blender until smooth. Return soup to saucepan; stir in half-and-half. Cook until heated through, stirring occasionally.

Pumpkin and Parmesan Twice-Baked Potatoes

MAKES 4 SERVINGS

2 baking potatoes (about 12 ounces each)

1 cup shredded Parmesan cheese

6 tablespoons half-and-half

¼ cup canned pumpkin

1½ teaspoons minced fresh sage or ¼ teaspoon dried sage

¼ teaspoon salt

⅛ teaspoon black pepper

1. Preheat oven to 400°F. Scrub potatoes; pierce in several places with fork or small knife. Place potatoes directly on oven rack; bake 1 hour or until soft.

2. When cool enough to handle, cut potatoes in half lengthwise. Scoop out most of potato pulp into medium bowl, leaving thin potato shell. Mash potatoes with fork. Add cheese, half-and-half, pumpkin, sage, salt and pepper; mix well.

3. Place potato shells on baking sheet; spoon pumpkin mixture into shells. Bake 10 minutes or until filling is heated through.

Creamy Pumpkin Baked Penne
MAKES 9 SERVINGS

1 package (14½ ounces) uncooked multigrain penne

1 tablespoon olive oil

1 small onion, chopped

3 cloves garlic, minced

1 can (28 ounces) crushed tomatoes

1 can (15 ounces) solid-pack pumpkin

¾ cup ricotta cheese

½ cup chicken broth

1 tablespoon Italian seasoning

1 teaspoon salt

¾ teaspoon red pepper flakes

1 cup (4 ounces) shredded mozzarella cheese

⅓ cup grated Parmesan cheese

1. Preheat oven to 375°F. Spray 13×9-inch baking dish with nonstick cooking spray. Cook pasta according to package directions until al dente.

2. Meanwhile, heat oil in large saucepan over medium-high heat. Add onion and garlic; cook and stir 3 minutes. Add tomatoes, pumpkin, ricotta, broth, Italian seasoning, salt and red pepper flakes; bring to a boil. Reduce heat to medium-low; cook, uncovered, 5 minutes, stirring occasionally. Add pasta; stir until coated with sauce. Spoon into prepared baking dish; sprinkle with mozzarella and Parmesan.

3. Bake 30 to 35 minutes or until cheeses are golden brown.

Pumpkin Risotto

MAKES 4 SERVINGS

4 cups (32 ounces) vegetable or chicken broth

5 whole fresh sage leaves

¼ teaspoon ground nutmeg

2 tablespoons butter

1 tablespoon olive oil

1 onion, finely chopped

2 cloves garlic, minced

1½ cups uncooked arborio rice

½ cup dry white wine

1 teaspoon salt

Black pepper

1 can (15 ounces) solid-pack pumpkin

½ cup shredded Parmesan cheese

2 tablespoons chopped fresh sage, divided

¼ cup roasted pumpkin seeds (pepitas) or chopped toasted walnuts or pecans

1. Combine broth, whole sage leaves and nutmeg in small saucepan; bring to a boil over high heat. Reduce heat to maintain a simmer.

2. Heat butter and oil in large saucepan over medium-high heat. Add onion; cook and stir 5 minutes or until softened. Add garlic; cook and stir 30 seconds. Add rice; cook 2 to 3 minutes or until rice appears translucent, stirring frequently to coat with butter. Add wine, salt and pepper; cook until most of liquid is absorbed.

3. Add broth, ½ cup at a time, stirring frequently until broth is absorbed before adding next ½ cup (discard whole sage leaves). Stir in pumpkin when about 1 cup broth remains. Add remaining broth; cook until rice is al dente, stirring constantly.

4. Remove from heat; stir in cheese and 1 tablespoon chopped sage. Cover and let stand 5 minutes. Top each serving with 1 tablespoon pumpkin seeds and remaining chopped sage.

Pumpkin Chile Cheese Dip

MAKES ABOUT 2 CUPS

1 tablespoon butter

¼ cup finely chopped green bell pepper

2 tablespoons finely chopped onion

1 can (10¾ ounces) condensed nacho cheese soup,* undiluted

1 cup canned pumpkin

½ cup half-and-half

1 to 2 teaspoons minced canned chipotle peppers in adobo sauce (see Note)

¼ teaspoon salt

Tortilla chips and/or vegetables

If nacho cheese soup is unavailable, substitute Cheddar cheese soup and add additional ½ teaspoon chipotle pepper.

1. Melt butter in medium saucepan over medium heat. Add bell pepper and onion; cook and stir 3 minutes or until tender.

2. Stir in soup, pumpkin, half-and-half, 1 teaspoon chipotle pepper and salt; cook over low heat 10 minutes, stirring frequently. Taste and add additional chipotle pepper, if desired. Serve warm with tortilla chips and/or vegetables for dipping.

 note Two teaspoons of chipotle pepper will make the dip very spicy. Start with 1 teaspoon and taste before adding the additional chipotle pepper.

Cookies & Bars

Pumpkin Whoopie Minis

MAKES ABOUT 2½ DOZEN SANDWICH COOKIES

1¾ cups all-purpose flour

2 teaspoons pumpkin pie spice

1 teaspoon baking powder

1 teaspoon baking soda

1 teaspoon salt, divided

1 cup packed brown sugar

½ cup (1 stick) butter, softened, divided

1 cup canned pumpkin

2 eggs, lightly beaten

¼ cup vegetable oil

1 teaspoon vanilla, divided

4 ounces cream cheese, softened

1½ cups powdered sugar

1. Preheat oven to 350°F. Line cookie sheets with parchment paper. Combine flour, pumpkin pie spice, baking powder, baking soda and ¾ teaspoon salt in medium bowl; mix well.

2. Beat brown sugar and ¼ cup butter in large bowl with electric mixer at medium speed until creamy. Add pumpkin, eggs, oil and ½ teaspoon vanilla; beat until well blended. Beat in flour mixture at low speed just until blended. Drop dough by teaspoonfuls 2 inches apart onto prepared cookie sheets.

3. Bake 10 to 12 minutes or until tops spring back when lightly touched. Cool on cookie sheets 5 minutes; remove to wire racks to cool completely.

4. Meanwhile, prepare filling. Beat cream cheese and remaining ¼ cup butter in medium bowl with electric mixer at medium speed until smooth and creamy. Beat in remaining ½ teaspoon vanilla and ¼ teaspoon salt until blended. Gradually add powdered sugar; beat until light and fluffy.

5. Pipe or spread heaping teaspoon filling on flat side of half of cookies; top with remaining cookies. Store cookies in airtight container in refrigerator.

Pumpkin Cheesecake Bars

MAKES 2 DOZEN BARS

1½ cups gingersnap crumbs, plus additional for garnish

6 tablespoons (¾ stick) butter, melted

2 eggs

¼ cup plus 2 tablespoons sugar, divided

2½ teaspoons vanilla, divided

11 ounces cream cheese, softened

1¼ cups canned pumpkin

1 teaspoon ground cinnamon

¼ teaspoon ground ginger

¼ teaspoon ground nutmeg

¼ teaspoon ground cloves

1 cup sour cream

1. Preheat oven to 325°F. Spray 13×9-inch baking pan with nonstick cooking spray.

2. Combine 1½ cups gingersnap crumbs and butter in small bowl; mix well. Press into bottom of prepared pan. Bake 10 minutes.

3. Meanwhile, combine eggs, ¼ cup sugar and 1½ teaspoons vanilla in food processor or blender; process 1 minute or until smooth. Add cream cheese and pumpkin; process until well blended. Stir in cinnamon, ginger, nutmeg and cloves. Pour evenly over hot crust.

4. Bake 40 minutes. Whisk sour cream, remaining 2 tablespoons sugar and 1 teaspoon vanilla in small bowl until blended. Remove cheesecake from oven; spread sour cream mixture over top. Bake 5 minutes. Turn off oven; open door halfway and let cheesecake cool completely in oven. Refrigerate at least 2 hours before serving. Garnish with additional gingersnap crumbs.

Pumpkin Raisin Cookies

MAKES ABOUT 3½ DOZEN COOKIES

½ cup (1 stick) butter, softened

1 cup packed brown sugar

½ cup granulated sugar

1½ cups canned pumpkin

1 egg

1 teaspoon vanilla

2¼ cups all-purpose flour

1¼ teaspoons ground cinnamon

1 teaspoon baking powder

½ teaspoon baking soda

½ teaspoon salt

½ teaspoon ground nutmeg

¾ cup raisins

½ cup chopped walnuts

Powdered Sugar Glaze (recipe follows)

1. Preheat oven to 350°F.

2. Beat butter, brown sugar and granulated sugar in large bowl with electric mixer at medium speed until creamy. Add pumpkin, egg and vanilla; beat until light and fluffy. Add flour, cinnamon, baking powder, baking soda, salt and nutmeg; beat at low speed until blended. Stir in raisins and walnuts. Drop dough by heaping tablespoonfuls 2 inches apart onto ungreased cookie sheets.

3. Bake 12 to 15 minutes or until set. Cool on cookie sheets 2 minutes; remove to wire racks to cool completely.

4. Prepare Powdered Sugar Glaze. Drizzle glaze over cookies; let stand until set. Store cookies in airtight container between layers of waxed paper.

Powdered Sugar Glaze: Combine 1 cup powdered sugar and 2 tablespoons milk in small bowl; whisk until smooth.

Pumpkin White Chocolate Drops

MAKES ABOUT 3 DOZEN COOKIES

1 cup granulated sugar

1 cup (2 sticks) butter, softened

½ (15-ounce) can solid-pack pumpkin

1 egg

2 cups all-purpose flour

1 teaspoon pumpkin pie spice*

½ teaspoon baking powder

¼ teaspoon baking soda

1 cup white chocolate chips

1 cup prepared cream cheese frosting

*Or substitute ½ teaspoon ground cinnamon, ¼ teaspoon ground ginger and ⅛ teaspoon each ground allspice and ground nutmeg.

1. Preheat oven to 375°F. Line cookie sheets with parchment paper or spray with nonstick cooking spray.

2. Beat granulated sugar and butter in large bowl with electric mixer at medium speed until light and fluffy. Add pumpkin and egg; beat until well blended. Add flour, pumpkin pie spice, baking powder and baking soda; beat at low speed just until blended. Stir in white chips. Drop dough by tablespoonfuls about 2 inches apart onto prepared cookie sheets.

3. Bake 16 minutes or until set and lightly browned. Cool on cookie sheets 1 minute; remove to wire racks to cool completely.

4. Spread frosting over cookies.

Whole Wheat Pumpkin Bars

MAKES 2 DOZEN BARS

1 cup all-purpose flour

1 cup whole wheat flour

¾ cup granulated sugar

1½ teaspoons baking powder

1½ teaspoons ground cinnamon

1 teaspoon baking soda

¾ teaspoon salt

½ teaspoon ground ginger

½ teaspoon ground nutmeg

1 can (15 ounces) solid-pack pumpkin

¾ cup canola oil

2 eggs

2 tablespoons molasses

Cream Cheese Frosting (recipe follows)

½ cup mini semisweet chocolate chips

1. Preheat oven to 350°F. Spray 13×9-inch baking pan with nonstick cooking spray.

2. Combine all-purpose flour, whole wheat flour, sugar, baking powder, cinnamon, baking soda, salt, ginger and nutmeg in medium bowl; mix well. Whisk pumpkin, oil, eggs and molasses in large bowl until well blended. Add flour mixture; stir until blended. Spread batter in prepared pan. (Batter will be very thick.)

3. Bake 20 to 25 minutes or until toothpick inserted into center comes out clean. Cool completely in pan on wire rack.

4. Prepare Cream Cheese Frosting. Spread frosting over bars; sprinkle with chocolate chips.

Cream Cheese Frosting: Beat 4 ounces softened cream cheese and ½ cup (1 stick) softened butter in medium bowl with electric mixer at medium-high speed until creamy. Add 2 cups powdered sugar; beat at low speed until blended. Add 1 tablespoon milk; beat at medium-high speed 2 to 3 minutes or until frosting is light and fluffy.

Maple-Pumpkin Gingerbread Cookies

MAKES 3 DOZEN COOKIES

¼ cup (½ stick) butter, softened

¼ cup packed brown sugar

1 egg

2 tablespoons molasses

½ cup plus 1½ tablespoons maple syrup, divided

½ cup canned pumpkin

¼ cup water

3⅓ cups all-purpose flour

1½ teaspoons ground ginger

1 teaspoon baking soda

½ teaspoon salt

½ teaspoon ground cinnamon

½ teaspoon ground cloves

¼ teaspoon ground nutmeg

¼ teaspoon ground black pepper

3 ounces cream cheese, softened

¾ cup powdered sugar

Milk as needed

1. Beat butter and brown sugar in large bowl with electric mixer at medium speed until fluffy. Beat in egg until blended. Add molasses, ½ cup maple syrup, pumpkin and water; beat until well blended.

2. Sift flour, ginger, baking soda, salt, cinnamon, cloves, nutmeg and pepper into medium bowl. Add to pumpkin mixture; beat at low speed just until blended. Shape dough into two discs; wrap each with plastic wrap. Refrigerate at least 4 hours or overnight.

3. Preheat oven to 350°F. Line cookie sheets with parchment paper. Roll out half of dough to ¼-inch thickness on lightly floured surface. Cut out circles with 3-inch round cookie cutter; place 1 inch apart on prepared cookie sheets. Repeat with remaining dough. Re-roll dough scraps once.

4. Bake 15 to 17 minutes or until edges are lightly browned. Cool on cookie sheets 5 minutes; remove to wire racks to cool completely.

5. Meanwhile, place cream cheese in food processor; process until smooth. Add powdered sugar and remaining 1½ tablespoons maple syrup; process until smooth. Add enough milk to reach spreadable consistency. Pipe or drizzle icing over cookies. Store covered in refrigerator.

Pumpkin Biscotti

MAKES ABOUT 28 BISCOTTI

5 cups all-purpose flour

1 tablespoon baking powder

1½ teaspoons salt

1 teaspoon ground cinnamon

½ teaspoon ground ginger

Dash ground cloves

1¼ cups plus 2 tablespoons sugar

1 cup (2 sticks) butter, softened

½ (15-ounce) can solid-pack pumpkin

2 tablespoons water

1 cup dried cranberries

½ cup chopped pistachio nuts (optional)

½ cup prepared cream cheese frosting

1. Preheat oven to 375°F. Line cookie sheets with parchment paper.

2. Combine flour, baking powder, salt, cinnamon, ginger and cloves in medium bowl. Beat sugar and butter in large bowl with electric mixer at medium speed until fluffy. Add pumpkin and water; beat until well blended. Gradually add flour mixture, beating at low speed until blended. Stir in cranberries and pistachios, if desired.

3. Shape dough into 2 logs, each about 14 inches long and 4 to 5 inches wide, on prepared cookie sheets.

4. Bake about 40 minutes or until firm to the touch. Remove cookie sheets to wire racks to cool 20 minutes. Transfer logs to cutting board; cut into 1-inch-thick slices. Arrange slices on cookie sheets, cut sides up; bake 20 minutes or until dry and lightly browned. Remove to wire racks to cool completely.

5. Place frosting in small microwavable bowl; microwave on HIGH 30 seconds or until melted. Drizzle over biscotti.

Pies & Tarts

Pumpkin Pecan Pie

MAKES 8 TO 10 SERVINGS

1 can (15 ounces) solid-pack pumpkin

1 can (14 ounces) sweetened condensed milk

¼ cup (½ stick) butter, softened

2 eggs, divided

1 teaspoon ground cinnamon

1 teaspoon vanilla

½ teaspoon ground nutmeg

¼ teaspoon salt

1 (6-ounce) graham cracker pie crust

2 tablespoons packed brown sugar

2 tablespoons dark corn syrup

1 tablespoon butter, melted

½ teaspoon maple flavoring

1 cup chopped pecans

Whipped cream (optional)

1. Preheat oven to 400°F.

2. Combine pumpkin, sweetened condensed milk, softened butter, 1 egg, cinnamon, vanilla, nutmeg and salt in large bowl; beat until well blended. Pour into pie crust.

3. Bake 20 minutes. Meanwhile, beat remaining egg, brown sugar, corn syrup, melted butter and maple flavoring in medium bowl until well blended. Stir in pecans.

4. Remove pie from oven; top with pecan mixture. *Reduce oven temperature to 350°F.* Bake 25 minutes or until knife inserted near center comes out clean. Cool completely on wire rack. Top with whipped cream, if desired.

Hidden Pumpkin Pies

MAKES 6 SERVINGS

1½ cups canned pumpkin

1 cup evaporated milk

2 eggs

¼ cup sugar

1¼ teaspoons vanilla, divided

1 teaspoon pumpkin pie spice*

3 egg whites

¼ teaspoon cream of tartar

⅓ cup honey

*Or substitute ½ teaspoon ground cinnamon, ¼ teaspoon ground ginger and ⅛ teaspoon each ground allspice and ground nutmeg.

1. Preheat oven to 350°F.

2. Combine pumpkin, evaporated milk, eggs, sugar, 1 teaspoon vanilla and pumpkin pie spice in large bowl; mix well. Pour into 6 (6-ounce) custard cups or soufflé dishes. Place in shallow baking dish or pan; pour boiling water around custard cups to depth of 1 inch.

3. Bake 25 minutes or until set. Meanwhile, combine egg whites, cream of tartar and remaining ¼ teaspoon vanilla in medium bowl; beat with electric mixer at high speed until soft peaks form. Gradually add honey, beating until stiff peaks form.

4. Spread egg white mixture over tops of hot pumpkin pies. Bake 8 to 12 minutes or until tops of pies are golden brown. Let stand 10 minutes. Serve warm.

Pumpkin Ice Cream Pie
with Caramel Sauce
MAKES 8 SERVINGS

25 gingersnap cookies, finely crushed (about 1½ cups)

¼ cup (½ stick) butter, melted

2 tablespoons granulated sugar

1 quart pumpkin ice cream, softened

1 cup packed dark brown sugar

½ cup whipping cream

6 tablespoons (¾ stick) butter, cut into pieces

¼ cup light corn syrup

½ teaspoon salt

1 cup chopped pecans, toasted*

To toast pecans, spread on baking sheet. Bake in preheated 350°F oven 6 to 8 minutes or until golden brown, stirring frequently.

1. Preheat oven to 350°F. Spray 9-inch pie plate with nonstick cooking spray.

2. Combine cookie crumbs, melted butter and granulated sugar in medium bowl; mix well. Press onto bottom and up side of prepared pie plate. Bake 8 minutes. Cool completely on wire rack.

3. Spread ice cream evenly in crust. Cover and freeze 1 hour.

4. Whisk brown sugar, cream, cubed butter, corn syrup and salt in medium saucepan over medium-high heat until sugar is dissolved. Boil 1 minute without stirring. Remove from heat; cool completely. Drizzle caramel sauce over pie; sprinkle with pecans.

Praline Pumpkin Tart

MAKES 8 SERVINGS

1¼ cups all-purpose flour

1 tablespoon granulated sugar

¾ teaspoon salt, divided

¼ cup cold shortening, cut into small pieces

¼ cup (½ stick) cold butter, cut into small pieces

3 to 4 tablespoons cold water

1 can (15 ounces) solid-pack pumpkin

1 can (12 ounces) evaporated milk

⅔ cup packed brown sugar

2 eggs

1 teaspoon ground cinnamon

½ teaspoon ground ginger

¼ teaspoon ground cloves

Praline Topping (recipe follows)

1. Combine flour, granulated sugar and ¼ teaspoon salt in large bowl; mix well. Cut in shortening and butter with pastry blender or two knives until coarse crumbs form. Sprinkle flour mixture with water, 1 tablespoon at a time, stirring with fork until dough holds together. Shape dough into a ball; wrap with plastic wrap. Refrigerate about 1 hour or until chilled.

2. Roll out dough into 13×9-inch rectangle on lightly floured surface. Press dough into bottom and up sides of 11×7-inch baking dish. Cover with plastic wrap; refrigerate 30 minutes.

3. Preheat oven to 400°F. Pierce crust with tines of fork at ¼-inch intervals. Line baking dish with foil; fill with dried beans, uncooked rice or ceramic pie weights.

4. Bake 10 minutes or until set. Remove foil lining and beans; bake 5 minutes or until crust is golden brown. Cool completely on wire rack.

5. Meanwhile, beat pumpkin, evaporated milk, brown sugar, eggs, cinnamon, remaining ½ teaspoon salt, ginger and cloves in large bowl with electric mixer at low speed until well blended. Pour into prepared crust. Bake 35 minutes.

6. Meanwhile, prepare Praline Topping. Sprinkle topping over tart. Bake 15 minutes or until knife inserted 1 inch from center comes out clean. Cool completely on wire rack.

Praline Topping: Combine ⅓ cup packed brown sugar, ⅓ cup chopped pecans and ⅓ cup quick oats in small bowl; mix well. Cut in 1 tablespoon softened butter with pastry blender or two knives until coarse crumbs form.

Ginger-Spiced Pumpkin Pie

MAKES 8 SERVINGS

1 cup finely crushed gingersnap cookies

¼ cup (½ stick) butter, melted

2 egg whites

¾ cup packed brown sugar

1 can (15 ounces) solid-pack pumpkin

1 cup evaporated milk

1 teaspoon vanilla

1 teaspoon ground ginger

1 teaspoon ground cinnamon

½ teaspoon salt

Additional gingersnap cookies, cut into quarters (optional)

1. Combine crushed cookies and butter in medium bowl; mix well. Press onto bottom and up side of 9-inch deep-dish pie plate. Refrigerate 30 minutes.

2. Preheat oven to 350°F. Whisk egg whites and brown sugar in large bowl until blended. Add pumpkin, evaporated milk, vanilla, ginger, cinnamon and salt; whisk until well blended. Pour into crust.

3. Bake 60 to 70 minutes or until center is set. Cool on wire rack 30 minutes. Serve warm or at room temperature. Garnish with additional cookies, if desired.

Golden Leaf Pumpkin Pie

MAKES 8 SERVINGS

1 package (15 ounces) refrigerated pie crusts (2 crusts), divided

1 can (15 ounces) solid-pack pumpkin

1 cup half-and-half

3 eggs

⅔ cup sugar

¼ cup honey

2 teaspoons ground cinnamon

1 teaspoon ground allspice

1 teaspoon ground nutmeg

½ teaspoon salt

½ teaspoon ground ginger

½ teaspoon ground cloves

Golden Leaves (recipe follows)

1. Preheat oven to 425°F.

2. Reserve one pie crust for Golden Leaves. Roll out remaining pie crust into 10-inch circle on lightly floured surface. Press into 9-inch pie plate; trim edge and flute.

3. Whisk pumpkin, half-and-half, eggs, sugar, honey, cinnamon, allspice, nutmeg, salt, ginger and cloves in large bowl until well blended. Pour into crust.

4. Bake 10 minutes. *Reduce oven temperature to 350°F.* Bake 40 to 45 minutes until crust is golden brown and knife inserted into center comes out clean. Cool completely on wire rack. Meanwhile, prepare Golden Leaves.

5. Arrange Golden Leaves on pie just before serving.

Golden Leaves: Roll out reserved pie crust to ⅛-inch thickness on lightly floured surface. Cut out leaf shapes with cookie cutters; place 1 inch apart on ungreased baking sheet. Brush leaves with ¼ cup half-and-half; sprinkle with 2 tablespoons sugar. Bake in 400°F oven 10 to 15 minutes or until golden brown. Remove to wire rack to cool completely.

Pumpkin Tartlets

MAKES 12 SERVINGS

1 refrigerated pie crust
(half of 15-ounce package)

1 can (15 ounces) solid-pack
pumpkin

¼ cup milk

1 egg

6 tablespoons sugar

¾ teaspoon ground cinnamon,
plus additional for topping

½ teaspoon vanilla

⅛ teaspoon salt

⅛ teaspoon ground nutmeg,
plus additional for topping

Dash ground allspice

1½ cups whipped topping

1. Preheat oven to 425°F. Spray 12 standard (2½-inch) muffin cups
with nonstick cooking spray.

2. Unroll pie crust on clean work surface. Cut out 12 circles with
2½-inch biscuit cutter; discard scraps. Press one circle into each
prepared muffin cup.

3. Whisk pumpkin, milk, egg, sugar, ¾ teaspoon cinnamon, vanilla, salt,
⅛ teaspoon nutmeg and allspice in medium bowl until well blended.
Spoon about 2 tablespoons pumpkin mixture into each tartlet shell.

4. Bake 10 minutes. *Reduce oven temperature to 325°F.* Bake 12 to
15 minutes or until knife inserted into centers comes out clean.
Remove to wire racks to cool completely.

5. Spoon 2 tablespoons whipped topping on each tartlet just before
serving. Sprinkle with additional cinnamon and/or nutmeg, if desired.

Cakes &
Cheesecakes

Pumpkin Spice Cake

MAKES 16 SERVINGS

1¾ cups all-purpose flour

¾ cup packed brown sugar

2 teaspoons ground cinnamon

1¾ teaspoons baking powder

1 teaspoon baking soda

1 teaspoon salt

1 teaspoon ground ginger

¼ teaspoon ground nutmeg

¼ teaspoon ground cloves

1 can (15 ounces) solid-pack pumpkin

4 eggs

⅔ cup vegetable or canola oil

1 cup raisins

Powdered sugar (optional)

1. Preheat oven to 350°F. Spray 13×9-inch baking pan with nonstick cooking spray.

2. Combine flour, brown sugar, cinnamon, baking powder, baking soda, salt, ginger, nutmeg and cloves in large bowl; mix well. Add pumpkin, eggs and oil; beat with electric mixer at medium speed 1 minute or until well blended. Stir in raisins. Pour batter into prepared pan.

3. Bake about 30 minutes or until toothpick inserted into center comes out clean. Cool completely in pan on wire rack. Sprinkle with powdered sugar just before serving, if desired.

Marbled Pumpkin Cheesecake

MAKES 12 TO 15 SERVINGS

Gingersnap Cookie Crust
(recipe follows)

4 packages (8 ounces each)
cream cheese, softened

½ cup sugar

6 eggs

1 cup sour cream

1 cup canned pumpkin

2 tablespoons all-purpose flour

2 teaspoons ground cinnamon

½ teaspoon ground ginger

½ teaspoon ground allspice

3 ounces semisweet chocolate,
melted

1. Prepare Gingersnap Cookie Crust.

2. *Increase oven temperature to 425°F.* Beat cream cheese in large bowl with electric mixer at medium-high speed about 3 minutes or until light and fluffy. Add sugar; beat until well blended. Add eggs, one at a time, beating well after each addition. Add sour cream, pumpkin, flour, cinnamon, ginger and allspice; beat until well blended.

3. Pour 2 cups batter into small bowl; stir in melted chocolate until well blended. Pour remaining batter into prepared crust. Spoon chocolate batter in large swirls over pumpkin batter; draw knife through batter to marbleize.

4. Bake 15 minutes. *Reduce oven temperature to 300°F.* Bake 45 minutes (center of cheesecake will not be set). Turn off oven; let cheesecake stand in oven with door slightly ajar 1 hour. Cool to room temperature on wire rack. Cover and refrigerate overnight.

5. Remove side of pan from cheesecake; place cheesecake on serving plate.

Gingersnap Cookie Crust: Preheat oven to 350°F. Combine 1 cup gingersnap cookie crumbs, ½ cup graham cracker crumbs and ¼ cup sugar in small bowl; mix well. Stir in 5 tablespoons melted butter until well blended. Press into bottom and ½ inch up side of 9-inch springform pan. Bake 8 minutes. Cool completely on wire rack.

Cider-Glazed Pumpkin Bundt Cakes

MAKES 10 CAKES

1 package (about 15 ounces) spice cake mix

1 can (15 ounces) solid-pack pumpkin

3 eggs

⅔ cup water

⅓ cup vegetable oil

4 cups plus 2 tablespoons apple cider, divided

16 whole cloves

½ teaspoon ground cinnamon

1½ teaspoons cornstarch

1. Preheat oven to 350°F. Grease and flour 10 mini (1-cup) bundt pan cups.

2. Combine cake mix, pumpkin, eggs, water and oil in large bowl; beat until well blended. Spoon batter evenly into prepared bundt pan cups (about ½ cup batter per cup).

3. Bake 30 minutes or until toothpick inserted near centers comes out clean. Cool in pans 15 minutes; invert onto wire racks to cool completely.

4. Meanwhile, combine 4 cups cider, cloves and cinnamon in large skillet; bring to a boil over high heat. Boil 7 minutes or until liquid has reduced to 1 cup. Whisk cornstarch into remaining 2 tablespoons cider in small bowl until smooth. Add to cider mixture; cook and stir until slightly thickened. Remove from heat; cool completely.

5. Remove and discard cloves. Spoon glaze over cakes.

Classic Pumpkin Roll
MAKES 10 SERVINGS

1   package (about 16 ounces)
     angel food cake mix

1¼ cups water

1¼ cups powdered sugar, divided

1   package (8 ounces) cream
     cheese, softened

1   container (8 ounces) thawed
     frozen whipped topping

½   cup canned pumpkin

     Cream Cheese Frosting
     (recipe follows)

½   cup chopped hazelnuts
     (optional)

1. Preheat oven to 350°F. Spray 17×12-inch jelly-roll pan with nonstick cooking spray. Line pan with parchment paper.

2. Beat cake mix and water according to package directions. Pour batter into prepared pan. Bake 17 minutes or until toothpick inserted into center comes out clean. Immediately invert cake onto clean towel sprinkled with ½ cup powdered sugar. Fold towel edge over cake edge; roll up cake and towel jelly-roll style into 12-inch-long roll. Place seam side down on wire rack to cool completely.

3. Beat cream cheese and remaining ¾ cup powdered sugar in large bowl with electric mixer at medium speed 2 minutes or until well blended and fluffy. Fold in whipped topping and pumpkin until blended. Refrigerate until ready to use. Prepare Cream Cheese Frosting.

4. Carefully unroll cake onto serving plate, removing towel. Spread pumpkin filling evenly over cake. Re-roll cake; place seam side down on plate. (If cake breaks, hold pieces together and roll as instructed. Breaks can later be hidden with frosting.) Frost with Cream Cheese Frosting; sprinkle with hazelnuts. Trim 1 inch off each end with serrated knife; discard scraps. Cover with plastic wrap; refrigerate 2 to 3 hours before serving.

Cream Cheese Frosting: Beat 2 packages (8 ounces each) softened cream cheese and ½ cup (1 stick) softened butter with electric mixer at medium-high speed 2 minutes or until well blended and fluffy. Add 2 cups powdered sugar, sifted, and 2 teaspoons vanilla; beat until well blended.

Southern-Style Pumpkin Cheesecake

MAKES 12 TO 15 SERVINGS

1¾ cups graham cracker crumbs

1 cup sugar, divided

½ cup (1 stick) butter, melted

1 package (8 ounces) cream cheese, softened

2 eggs, beaten

¾ cup milk

2 packages (4-serving size each) French vanilla instant pudding and pie filling mix

2 cups canned pumpkin

⅛ teaspoon ground cinnamon

1 container (12 ounces) thawed frozen whipped topping, divided

Dash ground nutmeg

1. Preheat oven to 350°F. Combine graham cracker crumbs, ¼ cup sugar and butter in small bowl; mix well. Press into bottom of 9-inch springform pan.

2. Beat cream cheese, eggs and remaining ¾ cup sugar in medium bowl with electric mixer at medium speed 2 minutes or until light and fluffy. Pour into crust.

3. Bake 20 minutes. Cool completely on wire rack.

4. Beat milk and pudding mix in large bowl with electric mixer at medium speed 2 minutes. Add pumpkin and cinnamon; beat until well blended. Fold in 1 cup whipped topping until blended. Spread pudding mixture over top of cheesecake; pipe or spoon remaining whipped topping over pudding layer. Sprinkle with nutmeg. Refrigerate 4 hours or overnight.

Pumpkin Pecan Cake

MAKES 12 TO 16 SERVINGS

---

1 can (15 ounces) solid-pack pumpkin

1 can (12 ounces) evaporated milk

1 cup packed brown sugar

3 eggs

2 teaspoons pumpkin pie spice

½ teaspoon salt

1 package (about 15 ounces) yellow cake mix

¾ cup (1½ sticks) butter, cut into thin slices

½ cup pecan halves

1. Preheat oven to 350°F. Spray 13×9-inch baking pan with nonstick cooking spray.

2. Whisk pumpkin, evaporated milk, brown sugar, eggs, pumpkin pie spice and salt in medium bowl until well blended. Pour into prepared pan; top with cake mix, spreading evenly. Top with butter in single layer, covering cake mix as much as possible. Sprinkle with pecans.

3. Bake about 1 hour or until toothpick inserted into center of cake comes out clean. Cool completely in pan on wire rack.

Celebration Pumpkin Cake

MAKES 12 SERVINGS

1 package (about 15 ounces)
   spice cake mix

1 can (15 ounces) solid-pack
   pumpkin

3 eggs

¼ cup (½ stick) butter, softened

1½ containers (16 ounces each)
   cream cheese frosting

⅓ cup caramel ice cream topping

   Pecan halves (optional)

1. Preheat oven to 350°F. Grease and flour three 9-inch round cake pans.

2. Beat cake mix, pumpkin, eggs and butter in large bowl with electric mixer at medium speed 2 minutes or until well blended. Pour batter into prepared pans.

3. Bake 20 minutes or until toothpick inserted into centers comes out clean. Cool in pans 15 minutes; remove to wire racks to cool completely.

4. Place one cake layer on serving plate; spread with one fourth of frosting. Repeat layers two times. Spread remaining frosting on side of cake. Spread caramel topping over top of cake, allowing some to drip down side. Garnish with pecans.

Pumpkin Spice Cupcakes
MAKES 24 CUPCAKES

1½ cups sugar

¾ cup (1½ sticks) butter, softened

3 eggs

1 can (15 ounces) solid-pack pumpkin

1 cup buttermilk

3 cups all-purpose flour

1 tablespoon baking powder

2 teaspoons ground cinnamon

1½ teaspoons baking soda

½ teaspoon salt

¼ teaspoon ground allspice

¼ teaspoon ground nutmeg

⅛ teaspoon ground ginger

Maple Frosting (recipe follows)

Colored decors or sugar (optional)

1. Preheat oven to 350°F. Line 24 standard (2½-inch) muffin cups with paper baking cups.

2. Beat sugar and butter in large bowl with electric mixer at medium speed 3 minutes or until light and fluffy. Add eggs, one at a time, beating well after each addition.

3. Whisk pumpkin and buttermilk in medium bowl until well blended. Combine flour, baking powder, cinnamon, baking soda, salt, allspice, nutmeg and ginger in separate medium bowl; mix well. Alternately add flour mixture and pumpkin mixture to butter mixture, beating well after each addition. Spoon batter evenly into prepared muffin cups.

4. Bake 20 minutes or until toothpick inserted into centers comes out clean. Cool in pans 10 minutes; remove to wire racks to cool completely.

5. Prepare Maple Frosting; pipe or spread onto cupcakes. Sprinkle with decors, if desired.

Maple Frosting: Beat ¾ cup (1½ sticks) softened butter in large bowl with electric mixer at medium speed until light and fluffy. Add 3 tablespoons maple syrup and ½ teaspoon vanilla; beat until well blended. Gradually add 3½ cups powdered sugar, beating until light and fluffy. Add 1 to 2 tablespoons milk, if necessary, to reach desired spreading consistency.

Delicious
Desserts

Pumpkin Crème Brûlée

MAKES 4 SERVINGS

1 cup whipping cream

1 cup half-and-half

½ cup granulated sugar

¼ teaspoon salt

¼ teaspoon ground cinnamon

Pinch ground nutmeg

4 egg yolks

½ cup canned pumpkin

4 tablespoons packed brown sugar

1. Preheat oven to 300°F. Spray 4 (1-cup) shallow ramekins or custard cups with nonstick cooking spray. Combine cream, half-and-half, granulated sugar, salt, cinnamon and nutmeg in medium saucepan; bring to a simmer over medium-high heat.

2. Beat egg yolks in heatproof bowl. Gradually whisk in one fourth of hot cream mixture. Slowly pour egg mixture back into remaining cream mixture in saucepan, whisking constantly until slightly thickened. Remove from heat; stir in pumpkin until well blended. Pour into prepared ramekins. Place ramekins in 9-inch square baking pan; place pan in oven. Pour hot water into baking pan to depth of 1 inch.

3. Bake 45 to 55 minutes or until set. Cool in pan 30 minutes. Remove ramekins from pan; refrigerate at least 1 hour.

4. Preheat broiler. Sprinkle 1 tablespoon brown sugar evenly over each custard. Place ramekins on baking sheet. Broil 4 inches from heat 1 minute or until sugar begins to bubble and turns golden brown. Cool 15 minutes before serving.

Pumpkin Bread Pudding

MAKES 2 SERVINGS

---

2 slices whole wheat bread

1 cup canned pumpkin

1 egg

2 tablespoons sugar

1 teaspoon vanilla

½ teaspoon ground cinnamon

1 tablespoon raisins

   Whipped topping (optional)

1. Preheat oven to 375°F. Spray 2 individual ovenproof baking dishes or custard cups with nonstick cooking spray.

2. Toast bread; cut into 1-inch cubes.

3. Whisk pumpkin, egg, sugar, vanilla and cinnamon in medium bowl until well blended. Fold in toast cubes and raisins. Divide mixture evenly between prepared baking dishes.

4. Bake 30 minutes. Serve warm with whipped topping, if desired.

Pumpkin Mousse
MAKES 6 SERVINGS

1 cup milk

1 package (4-serving size) butterscotch instant pudding and pie filling mix

1 can (15 ounces) solid-pack pumpkin

¼ teaspoon ground cinnamon

Pinch ground ginger

Pinch ground cloves

1 container (8 ounces) thawed frozen whipped topping, divided

2 tablespoons chopped crystallized ginger (optional)

1. Whisk milk and pudding mix in large bowl. Add pumpkin, cinnamon, ground ginger and cloves; whisk until well blended.

2. Reserve ¼ cup whipped topping for garnish. Fold remaining whipped topping into pudding mixture. Refrigerate 1 hour or until set.

3. Just before serving, top with reserved whipped topping and crystallized ginger, if desired.

Pumpkin Pie Pops

MAKES 6 POPS

½ cup canned pumpkin pie mix

½ cup milk

¼ teaspoon vanilla

1½ cups vanilla ice cream

6 (5-ounce) paper or plastic cups or pop molds

2 containers (4 ounces each) prepared refrigerated vanilla pudding, divided

3 teaspoons packed brown sugar, divided

6 whole cinnamon sticks or pop sticks

1. Combine pumpkin pie mix, milk and vanilla in blender or food processor; blend until smooth. Add ice cream; blend until smooth.

2. Pour 2 tablespoons mixture into each cup. Freeze 30 to 45 minutes or just until set. Cover and refrigerate remaining pumpkin mixture.

3. Combine 1 container vanilla pudding and 1½ teaspoons brown sugar; mix well. Spoon 1 tablespoon mixture over pumpkin mixture in each cup. Freeze 30 to 45 minutes or just until set.

4. Pour 2 tablespoons pumpkin mixture over pudding mixture in each cup. Freeze 30 to 45 minutes or just until set. Cover and refrigerate remaining pumpkin mixture.

5. Combine remaining 1 container pudding and 1½ teaspoons brown sugar; mix well. Spoon 1 tablespoon mixture over pumpkin mixture in each cup. Freeze 30 to 45 minutes or just until set.

6. Pour 1 tablespoon pumpkin mixture over pudding mixture in each cup. Cover top of each cup with small piece of foil. Freeze 30 to 45 minutes or just until set.

7. Gently insert cinnamon sticks through center of foil. Freeze 6 hours or until firm.

8. To serve, remove foil and peel away paper cups or gently twist frozen pops out of plastic cups.

Pumpkin Custard
MAKES 6 SERVINGS

1 can (15 ounces) solid-pack pumpkin

1 teaspoon pumpkin pie spice

⅛ teaspoon salt

¾ cup evaporated milk

3 eggs

¼ cup packed dark brown sugar

2 tablespoons chopped dried cherries

2 tablespoons granola

4 cups boiling water

1. Preheat oven to 350°F. Spray 6 (6-ounce) custard cups with nonstick cooking spray. Place cups in 13×9-inch baking pan.

2. Whisk pumpkin, pumpkin pie spice and salt in small bowl until well blended. Heat evaporated milk in small saucepan until steaming but not boiling. Meanwhile, whisk eggs and brown sugar in medium bowl until smooth. Gradually whisk hot milk into egg mixture. Whisk in pumpkin mixture until well blended. Spoon evenly into prepared cups; sprinkle with cherries and granola.

3. Place baking pan in oven; pour boiling water into pan until water reaches halfway up sides of custard cups.

4. Bake 25 to 30 minutes or until knife inserted into centers comes out clean. Remove cups to wire rack. Serve warm or chilled.

Pumpkin Cheesecake in Pastry

MAKES 6 SERVINGS

1 package frozen puff pastry shells (6 shells)

1 package (4-serving size) cheesecake or vanilla instant pudding and pie filling mix

1 cup milk

1 package (8 ounces) cream cheese, softened

½ (15-ounce) can solid-pack pumpkin

⅓ cup maple syrup

2 teaspoons ground cinnamon, plus additional for topping

1 teaspoon vanilla

¼ teaspoon ground nutmeg

¼ teaspoon ground allspice

1. Bake puff pastry shells according to package directions. Cool completely.

2. Meanwhile, combine pudding mix, milk, cream cheese, pumpkin, maple syrup, 2 teaspoons cinnamon, vanilla, nutmeg and allspice in food processor; process until smooth. Transfer to medium bowl; cover and refrigerate until ready to serve.

3. Just before serving, remove tops of pastry shells. Spoon about ½ cup pumpkin filling into each shell; sprinkle with additional cinnamon, if desired. Garnish with tops of pastry shells.

Caramel Pumpkin Flan

MAKES ABOUT 6 SERVINGS

¾ cup sugar, divided

4 eggs

1 cup canned pumpkin

1 teaspoon ground cinnamon

¼ teaspoon salt

¼ teaspoon ground ginger

¼ teaspoon ground allspice

¼ teaspoon ground nutmeg

1 cup half-and-half

½ teaspoon vanilla

1. Preheat oven to 350°F. Heat ½ cup sugar in medium skillet over medium heat until sugar is melted and golden brown, stirring constantly. Immediately pour caramel into 1-quart soufflé dish or 8-inch round baking dish. Tilt dish so caramel flows over bottom and slightly up side. Let stand 10 minutes.

2. Beat eggs in large bowl with electric mixer at medium speed 1 minute. Add remaining ¼ cup sugar, pumpkin, cinnamon, salt, ginger, allspice and nutmeg; beat until well blended. Add half-and-half and vanilla; beat until smooth. Pour over caramel. Place soufflé dish in larger pan; pour warm water into larger pan to depth of 1½ inches.

3. Bake 45 to 50 minutes or until knife inserted into center comes out clean. Remove soufflé dish from water; cool on wire rack. Cover loosely and refrigerate 6 hours or overnight.

4. To unmold, run knife around edge of dish. Cover with rimmed serving plate; invert and lift off dish. Cut flan into wedges; spoon caramel over top.

Sweet Potato
RECIPES

Breakfast & Brunch

Ham and Sweet Potato Skillet

MAKES 4 SERVINGS

3 cups water

2 sweet potatoes (about 1¼ pounds), peeled and cut into ¾-inch pieces

1 tablespoon salt

1 fully cooked ham steak (about 1 pound)

½ cup brewed coffee

¼ cup pure maple syrup

2 tablespoons butter

½ cup coarsely chopped pecans, toasted*

*To toast pecans, cook in medium skillet over medium-low heat about 5 minutes or until lightly browned, stirring frequently.

1. Combine water, sweet potatoes and salt in large saucepan; bring to a boil over medium heat. Reduce heat to medium-low; cook 8 to 10 minutes or until almost tender. Drain well.

2. Meanwhile, cut ham into ¾-inch pieces; discard bone and fat.

3. Combine coffee, maple syrup and butter in large skillet; bring to a boil over high heat. Reduce heat to medium-low; simmer 3 minutes. Add sweet potatoes and ham; cook until ham is heated through and sauce is bubbly and slightly thickened, stirring occasionally. Sprinkle with pecans just before serving.

Sweet Potato Muffins

MAKES 24 MUFFINS

2 cups all-purpose flour

¾ cup chopped walnuts

¾ cup golden raisins

½ cup packed brown sugar

1 tablespoon baking powder

1 teaspoon ground cinnamon

½ teaspoon salt

½ teaspoon baking soda

¼ teaspoon ground nutmeg

1 cup mashed cooked sweet potato

¾ cup milk

½ cup (1 stick) butter, melted

2 eggs, beaten

1½ teaspoons vanilla

1. Preheat oven to 400°F. Spray 24 standard (2½-inch) muffin cups with nonstick cooking spray or line with paper baking cups.

2. Combine flour, walnuts, raisins, brown sugar, baking powder, cinnamon, salt, baking soda and nutmeg in medium bowl; mix well.

3. Whisk sweet potato, milk, butter, eggs and vanilla in large bowl until well blended. Add flour mixture to sweet potato mixture; stir just until moistened. Spoon batter evenly into prepared muffin cups.

4. Bake 15 minutes or until toothpick inserted into centers comes out clean. Cool in pans 5 minutes; remove to wire racks to cool completely.

Sweet Potato and Turkey Sausage Hash

MAKES 2 SERVINGS

1 link mild or hot turkey Italian sausage (about 4 ounces)

2 teaspoons olive oil

1 small red onion, finely chopped

1 small red bell pepper, finely chopped

1 small sweet potato, peeled and cut into ½-inch cubes

¼ teaspoon salt

¼ teaspoon black pepper

⅛ teaspoon cumin

⅛ teaspoon chipotle chile powder

1. Remove sausage from casing; shape into ½-inch balls. Heat oil in large skillet over medium heat. Add sausage; cook and stir 3 to 5 minutes or until browned. Remove to plate.

2. Add onion, bell pepper, sweet potato, salt, black pepper, cumin and chipotle powder to skillet; cook and stir 5 to 8 minutes or until sweet potato is tender.

3. Add sausage; cook without stirring 5 minutes or until hash is lightly browned.

Sweet Potato Pancakes with Apple-Cherry Chutney

MAKES 6 SERVINGS

- 1 cup chunky applesauce
- ½ cup canned tart red cherries, drained
- 2 tablespoons sugar
- 1 teaspoon lemon juice
- ½ teaspoon ground cinnamon
- ⅛ teaspoon ground nutmeg
- 1 pound sweet potatoes (about 2 medium), peeled and cut into pieces

- ½ small onion
- 3 egg whites
- 2 tablespoons all-purpose flour
- ½ teaspoon salt
- ¼ teaspoon black pepper
- 4 teaspoons vegetable oil, divided

1. Combine applesauce, cherries, sugar, lemon juice, cinnamon and nutmeg in small saucepan; bring to a boil over medium heat. Reduce heat to low; cook 5 minutes, stirring occasionally. Set aside and keep warm.

2. Combine sweet potatoes, onion, egg whites, flour, salt and pepper in food processor or blender; process until almost smooth (mixture will appear grainy).

3. Heat 1 teaspoon oil in large nonstick skillet over medium heat 1 minute. Spoon ⅓ cup batter into skillet for each pancake. Cook 3 pancakes at a time, 3 minutes per side or until golden brown. Repeat with remaining oil and batter. Serve pancakes with chutney.

Sweet Potato Biscuits

MAKES ABOUT 12 BISCUITS

2½ cups all-purpose flour

¼ cup packed brown sugar

1 tablespoon baking powder

¾ teaspoon salt

¾ teaspoon ground cinnamon

¼ teaspoon ground ginger

¼ teaspoon ground allspice

½ cup shortening

½ cup chopped pecans

¾ cup mashed canned
sweet potatoes

½ cup milk

1. Preheat oven to 450°F.

2. Combine flour, brown sugar, baking powder, salt, cinnamon, ginger and allspice in medium bowl; mix well. Cut in shortening with pastry blender or two knives until mixture resembles coarse crumbs. Stir in pecans.

3. Whisk sweet potatoes and milk in small bowl until blended. Stir into flour mixture until soft dough forms. Turn out dough onto lightly floured surface; knead lightly. Roll out dough to ½-inch thickness. Cut out biscuits with 2½-inch round cutter. Place on ungreased baking sheet.

4. Bake 12 to 14 minutes or until golden brown. Serve warm.

Beefy Sweet Potato Hash

MAKES 4 SERVINGS

1 tablespoon butter

1 tablespoon all-purpose flour

⅓ cup beef broth

1 teaspoon Worcestershire sauce

1 pound leftover pot roast, roast beef or steak, diced

1 large sweet potato (about 12 ounces), peeled and diced

1 stalk celery, diced

1 cup corn

¼ cup diced red or green bell pepper

¼ cup (1 ounce) shredded Cheddar cheese (optional)

1. Melt butter in large skillet over medium heat. Whisk in flour; cook 2 minutes, stirring constantly. Whisk in broth and Worcestershire sauce; bring to a simmer. Stir in beef, sweet potato, celery, corn and bell pepper. Return to a simmer; cover and cook 12 minutes or until vegetables are tender.

2. Sprinkle cheese over hash just before serving, if desired.

Soups
&
Stews

Creamy Sweet Potato and Butternut Squash Soup

MAKES 4 TO 6 SERVINGS

1 pound sweet potatoes, peeled and cut into 1-inch pieces (about 3 cups)

1 pound butternut squash, peeled and cut into 1-inch pieces (about 3½ cups)

½ cup chopped onion

1 can (about 14 ounces) chicken broth, divided

½ cup (1 stick) butter, cubed

1 can (13½ ounces) coconut milk

1½ teaspoons salt

½ teaspoon ground cumin

½ teaspoon ground red pepper

3 to 4 green onions, finely chopped (optional)

Slow Cooker Directions

1. Combine sweet potatoes, squash, onion, half of broth and butter in slow cooker.

2. Cover; cook on HIGH 4 hours or until vegetables are tender.

3. Process soup in batches in food processor or blender until smooth. Return to slow cooker; stir in remaining broth, coconut milk, salt, cumin and red pepper. Cover; cook on HIGH until heated through. Sprinkle with green onions, if desired.

Chicken and Sweet Potato Chili

MAKES 4 SERVINGS

1 to 2 sweet potatoes, peeled and cut into ½-inch pieces

2 teaspoons canola oil

1 cup chopped onion

¾ pound boneless skinless chicken breasts or chicken tenders, cut into ¾-inch pieces*

3 cloves garlic, minced

2 teaspoons chili powder

1 can (about 14 ounces) diced fire-roasted tomatoes

1 can (about 15 ounces) kidney or pinto beans, drained and rinsed

½ cup chipotle or jalapeño salsa

*This is easier to do if chicken is partially frozen.

1. Place sweet potatoes in large saucepan; add water to cover. Bring to a boil over high heat. Reduce heat to medium-low; cook 5 minutes or until almost tender. Drain and set aside.

2. Heat oil in large saucepan over medium heat. Add onion; cook and stir 5 minutes. Add chicken, garlic and chili powder; cook 3 minutes, stirring frequently.

3. Add tomatoes, beans, salsa and sweet potatoes; bring to a boil over high heat. Reduce heat to low; cook, uncovered, 10 minutes or until chicken is cooked through.

Jerk Pork and Sweet Potato Stew

MAKES 4 SERVINGS

2 tablespoons all-purpose flour

¼ teaspoon salt

¼ teaspoon black pepper

1¼ pounds boneless pork shoulder, cut into bite-size pieces

2 tablespoons vegetable oil

1 large sweet potato, peeled and diced

1 cup corn

4 tablespoons minced green onions, divided

1 clove garlic, minced

½ medium Scotch bonnet or jalapeño pepper,* seeded and minced

⅛ teaspoon ground allspice

1 cup chicken broth

1 tablespoon lime juice

Hot cooked rice

Scotch bonnet and jalapeño peppers can sting and irritate the skin, so wear rubber gloves when handling and do not touch your eyes.

Slow Cooker Directions

1. Combine flour, salt and pepper in large resealable food storage bag. Add pork; shake well to coat. Heat oil in large skillet over medium heat. Working in batches, add pork in single layer and cook about 5 minutes or until browned on all sides. Transfer to slow cooker.

2. Add sweet potato, corn, 2 tablespoons green onions, garlic, Scotch bonnet pepper and allspice. Stir in broth.

3. Cover; cook on LOW 5 to 6 hours. Stir in lime juice and remaining 2 tablespoons green onions. Serve with rice.

Sweet Potato and Ham Soup

MAKES 6 SERVINGS

1 tablespoon butter

1 leek, sliced

1 clove garlic, minced

4 cups reduced-sodium chicken broth

2 sweet potatoes, peeled and cut into ¾-inch pieces

½ pound ham, cut into ½-inch pieces

½ teaspoon dried thyme

2 ounces stemmed spinach, coarsely chopped

1. Melt butter in large saucepan over medium heat. Add leek and garlic; cook and stir until tender.

2. Add broth, sweet potatoes, ham and thyme; bring to a boil over high heat. Reduce heat to low; simmer 10 minutes or until sweet potatoes are tender.

3. Stir spinach into soup; cook 2 minutes or until wilted. Serve immediately.

Middle Eastern Vegetable Stew

MAKES 6 SERVINGS

¼ cup olive oil

3 cups (12 ounces) sliced zucchini

2 cups (6 ounces) cubed peeled eggplant

2 cups sliced quartered peeled sweet potatoes

1½ cups cubed peeled butternut squash (optional)

1 can (28 ounces) crushed tomatoes in purée

1 cup drained canned chickpeas

½ cup raisins or currants (optional)

1½ teaspoons ground cinnamon

1 teaspoon grated orange peel

¾ teaspoon ground cumin

½ teaspoon salt

½ teaspoon paprika

¼ to ½ teaspoon ground red pepper

⅛ teaspoon ground cardamom

Hot cooked whole wheat couscous or brown rice (optional)

1. Heat oil in large saucepan or Dutch oven over medium heat. Add zucchini, eggplant, sweet potatoes and butternut squash, if desired; cook and stir 8 to 10 minutes or until vegetables are slightly softened.

2. Stir in tomatoes, chickpeas, raisins, if desired, cinnamon, orange peel, cumin, salt, paprika, red pepper and cardamom; bring to a boil over high heat. Reduce heat to low; cover and cook 30 minutes or until vegetables are tender. If sauce becomes too thick, stir in water to thin. Serve over couscous, if desired.

Sweet Potato Bisque

MAKES 4 SERVINGS

1 pound sweet potatoes, peeled and cut into 2-inch pieces

1 tablespoon butter

½ cup finely chopped onion

1 teaspoon curry powder

½ teaspoon ground coriander

¼ teaspoon salt

⅔ cup unsweetened apple juice

1 cup buttermilk

¼ cup water

Fresh snipped chives (optional)

Plain yogurt (optional)

1. Place sweet potatoes in large saucepan; add water to cover. Bring to a boil over high heat. Reduce heat to medium; cook 15 minutes or until potatoes are fork-tender. Drain and cool under cold running water.

2. Meanwhile, melt butter in small saucepan over medium heat. Add onion; cook and stir 2 minutes. Add curry powder, coriander and salt; cook and stir 1 minute or until onion is tender. Remove from heat; stir in apple juice.

3. Combine sweet potatoes, buttermilk and onion mixture in food processor or blender; process until smooth. Return to saucepan; stir in ¼ cup water, if neccesary, to thin to desired consistency. Cook and stir over medium heat until heated through. *Do not boil.* Garnish with chives or dollop of yogurt.

Spicy African Chickpea and Sweet Potato Stew

MAKES 4 SERVINGS

Spice Paste (recipe follows)

1½ pounds sweet potatoes, peeled and diced

2 cups vegetable broth or water

1 can (about 15 ounces) chickpeas, rinsed and drained

1 can (about 14 ounces) plum tomatoes, undrained, chopped

1½ cups sliced fresh okra or 1 package (10 ounces) frozen cut okra, thawed

1 tablespoon olive oil

5 green onions, sliced

1⅔ cups water

½ teaspoon salt

⅛ teaspoon saffron threads or ½ teaspoon ground turmeric

1 cup uncooked couscous

Hot pepper sauce

Fresh cilantro (optional)

1. Prepare Spice Paste.

2. Combine sweet potatoes, broth, chickpeas, tomatoes with juice, okra and Spice Paste in large saucepan; bring to a boil over high heat. Reduce heat to low; cover and cook 15 minutes. Uncover; cook 10 minutes or until vegetables are tender.

3. Meanwhile, heat oil in medium saucepan over medium heat. Add green onions; cook and stir 4 minutes. Add water, salt and saffron; bring to a boil. Stir in couscous. Remove from heat; cover and let stand 5 minutes. Fluff couscous with fork before serving.

4. Serve stew with couscous and hot pepper sauce. Garnish with cilantro.

Spice Paste: Combine 6 cloves peeled garlic and 1 teaspoon coarse salt in blender or small food processor; blend until garlic is finely chopped. Add 2 teaspoons paprika, 1½ teaspoons whole cumin seeds, 1 teaspoon black pepper, ½ teaspoon ground ginger and ½ teaspoon ground allspice; blend 15 seconds. With blender running, pour in 1 tablespoon olive oil through cover opening; blend until mixture forms paste.

Chunky Black Bean and Sweet Potato Chili

MAKES 5 SERVINGS

2 teaspoons vegetable oil

1 cup chopped sweet onion

2 red or green bell peppers or 1 of each, cut into ½-inch pieces

4 cloves garlic, minced

1 teaspoon chili powder

1 can (about 14 ounces) fire-roasted diced tomatoes

1 small sweet potato (about 8 ounces), peeled and cut into ½-inch pieces (1½ cups)

1 tablespoon minced canned chipotle peppers in adobo sauce

1 can (about 15 ounces) black beans, rinsed and drained

½ cup chopped fresh cilantro (optional)

1. Heat oil in large saucepan over medium heat. Add onion; cook and stir 5 minutes. Add bell peppers, garlic and chili powder; cook and stir 2 minutes. Add tomatoes, sweet potato and chipotle peppers; bring to a boil. Reduce heat to medium-low; cover and cook 15 minutes.

2. Stir in beans; cover and cook 8 to 10 minutes or until vegetables are tender. (Chili will be thick; thin with water as desired.) Sprinkle with cilantro, if desired.

Beef Stew with Bacon, Onion and Sweet Potatoes

MAKES 4 SERVINGS

---

1 pound beef stew meat, cut into 1-inch pieces

1 can (about 14 ounces) beef broth

2 medium sweet potatoes, peeled and cut into 2-inch pieces

1 large onion, cut into 1½-inch pieces

2 slices thick-cut bacon, diced

1 teaspoon dried thyme

1 teaspoon salt

¼ teaspoon black pepper

2 tablespoons cornstarch

2 tablespoons water

Slow Cooker Directions

1. Spray inside of slow cooker with nonstick cooking spray. Combine beef, broth, potatoes, onion, bacon, thyme, salt and pepper in slow cooker.

2. Cover; cook on LOW 7 to 8 hours or on HIGH 4 to 5 hours. Transfer beef and vegetables to serving bowl with slotted spoon; keep warm.

3. Whisk cornstarch into water in small bowl until smooth. Stir into cooking liquid. Cover; cook on HIGH 15 minutes or until thickened. Spoon sauce over beef and vegetables.

Groundnut Soup with Ginger and Cilantro

MAKES 4 SERVINGS

1 tablespoon vegetable oil

1½ cups chopped onions

1 medium clove garlic, minced

2 teaspoons chili powder

1 teaspoon ground cumin

¼ teaspoon red pepper flakes

8 ounces sweet potatoes, peeled and cut into ½-inch pieces

3 cups chicken broth

1 can (about 14 ounces) diced tomatoes

1 medium carrot, peeled and cut into ½-inch pieces

2 teaspoons sugar

1 cup salted peanuts

1 tablespoon grated fresh ginger

¼ cup chopped fresh cilantro

1. Heat oil in large saucepan over medium-high heat. Add onions; cook and stir 4 minutes or until translucent. Add garlic, chili powder, cumin and red pepper flakes; cook and stir 15 seconds.

2. Add sweet potatoes, broth, tomatoes, carrot and sugar; bring to a boil over high heat. Reduce heat to low; cover and simmer 25 minutes or until vegetables are tender, stirring occasionally. Remove from heat; stir in peanuts and ginger. Cool slightly.

3. Working in batches, process soup in food processor or blender until smooth. Return to saucepan; heat over medium-high heat 2 minutes or until heated through. Sprinkle with cilantro.

Main
Dishes

Maple Salmon and Sweets

MAKES 4 SERVINGS

½ cup pure maple syrup

2 tablespoons butter, melted

1½ pounds skin-on salmon fillets

2 medium sweet potatoes,
  peeled and cut into
  ¼-inch slices

1 teaspoon salt

¼ teaspoon black pepper

1. Combine maple syrup and butter in small bowl; mix well. Place salmon in resealable food storage bag. Place sweet potatoes in another resealable food storage bag. Pour half of syrup mixture into each bag; seal bags and turn to coat. Refrigerate at least 2 hours or overnight, turning bags occasionally.

2. Prepare grill for direct cooking. Oil grid. Drain salmon and sweet potatoes; discard marinade. Season with salt and pepper.

3. Grill salmon, skin-side down, on covered grill over medium heat 15 to 20 minutes or until fish begins to flake when tested with fork. (Do not turn.) Grill sweet potatoes, covered, in single layer on grill topper 15 minutes or until tender and slightly browned, turning once or twice.

Spiraled Sweet Potato and Black Bean Tacos

MAKES 4 SERVINGS

¼ cup sour cream

2 tablespoons mayonnaise

Juice of 1 lime

½ teaspoon chipotle chili powder

1 can (about 15 ounces) black beans, undrained

1 teaspoon smoked paprika

1 sweet potato, peeled

1 red onion

1 green bell pepper

4 teaspoons vegetable oil, divided

¼ teaspoon salt

8 small taco-size tortillas

1 avocado, sliced

¼ cup chopped fresh cilantro

¼ cup grated cojita cheese

Lime wedges and salsa (optional)

1. Combine sour cream, mayonnaise, lime juice and chili powder in small bowl; mix well. Refrigerate until ready to use.

2. Combine beans with liquid and paprika in small saucepan; cook over medium-low heat 5 to 7 minutes or until heated through, stirring occasionally. Remove from heat; coarsely mash beans with potato masher, leaving some beans whole. Keep warm.

3. Spiral sweet potatoes with medium spiral blade; cut into desired lengths. Spiral onion with fine spiral blade and bell pepper with spiral slicing blade; cut into desired lengths.

4. Heat 2 teaspoons oil in large nonstick skillet over medium heat. Add sweet potato; cook and stir 7 to 10 minutes or until tender. Remove to bowl; sprinkle with salt.

5. Heat remaining 2 teaspoons oil in same skillet over high heat. Add onion and bell pepper; cook and stir 5 minutes or until vegetables are softened and browned.

6. Spread beans down center of each tortilla. Top with sweet potatoes, vegetables, sour cream mixture, avocado, cilantro and cheese; fold in half. Serve with lime wedges and salsa, if desired.

Sweet and Savory Brisket

MAKES 8 SERVINGS

1 large onion, thinly sliced

1 small (2 to 2½ pounds) well-trimmed beef brisket

½ teaspoon salt

½ teaspoon black pepper

⅔ cup chili sauce, divided

1½ tablespoons packed brown sugar

¼ teaspoon ground cinnamon

2 large sweet potatoes, peeled and cut into 1-inch pieces

1 cup (5 ounces) pitted prunes

2 tablespoons cornstarch

2 tablespoons cold water

Slow Cooker Directions

1. Place onion in slow cooker. Arrange brisket over onion (tucking edges under to fit, if necessary). Sprinkle with salt and pepper; top with ⅓ cup chili sauce.

2. Cover; cook on HIGH 3½ hours. Combine remaining ⅓ cup chili sauce, brown sugar and cinnamon in large bowl; mix well. Add sweet potatoes and prunes; toss to coat. Spoon mixture over brisket. Cover; cook on HIGH 1¼ to 1½ hours or until brisket and sweet potatoes are tender.

3. Transfer brisket to cutting board; tent with foil. Transfer sweet potato mixture to serving platter, leaving juices in slow cooker. Keep warm.

4. Blend cornstarch into water in small bowl until smooth. Stir mixture into slow cooker juices. Cover; cook on HIGH 10 minutes or until sauce thickens.

5. Cut brisket against the grain into thin slices. Serve with sweet potato mixture and sauce.

Pork Cutlets with Sweet Potatoes and Onions

MAKES 2 SERVINGS

2 teaspoons olive oil, divided

½ yellow onion, peeled and sliced

2 medium sweet potatoes, cooked, peeled and diced (⅓-inch cubes)

⅛ teaspoon ground allspice

⅛ teaspoon ground cinnamon

¼ teaspoon black pepper

⅛ teaspoon onion powder

2 boneless pork loin cutlets

1. Heat 1 teaspoon oil in large nonstick skillet over medium-high heat. Add onion; cook and stir 3 minutes or until translucent. Add sweet potatoes, allspice and cinnamon; cook 5 minutes or until sweet potatoes are lightly browned, stirring occasionally. Remove to plate; keep warm.

2. Sprinkle black pepper and onion powder over both sides of pork. Heat remaining 1 teaspoon oil in same skillet over medium heat. Add pork; cook 3 minutes per side or until cooked through. Serve with vegetables.

Smoked Paprika Drumsticks with Roasted Sweet Potatoes

MAKES 4 SERVINGS

2 teaspoons smoked paprika

1 teaspoon ground cumin

1 teaspoon garlic powder

¾ teaspoon black pepper

½ teaspoon salt

4 (4-ounce) chicken drumsticks, skin removed

12 ounces sweet potatoes, peeled and cut into 1-inch pieces

1 medium onion, cut into 8 wedges

1 tablespoon extra virgin olive oil

1. Preheat oven to 350°F. Line large rimmed baking sheet with foil.

2. Combine paprika, cumin, garlic powder, pepper and salt in small bowl; coat chicken with mixture. Place chicken on prepared baking sheet.

3. Combine sweet potatoes, onion and oil in medium bowl; toss to coat. Arrange vegetables around chicken, being careful not to crowd.

4. Roast 30 minutes. Stir vegetables and turn chicken; roast 20 minutes or until chicken is cooked through (165°F).

Quinoa with Roasted Vegetables

MAKES 6 SERVINGS

2 medium sweet potatoes,
  cut into ½-inch-thick slices

1 medium eggplant, peeled
  and cut into ½-inch pieces

1 medium tomato, cut into
  wedges

1 large green bell pepper, sliced

1 small onion, cut into wedges

4 teaspoons olive oil, divided

½ teaspoon salt

¼ teaspoon black pepper

¼ teaspoon ground red pepper

1 cup uncooked quinoa

2 cloves garlic, minced

½ teaspoon dried thyme

¼ teaspoon dried marjoram

2 cups water or vegetable broth

1. Preheat oven to 450°F. Line large rimmed baking sheet with foil.

2. Combine sweet potatoes, eggplant, tomato, bell pepper, onion, 1 tablespoon oil, salt, black pepper and red pepper on prepared baking sheet; toss to coat. Spread vegetables in single layer.

3. Roast 20 to 30 minutes or until vegetables are browned and tender.

4. Meanwhile, place quinoa in fine-mesh strainer; rinse well under cold running water. Heat remaining 1 teaspoon oil in medium saucepan over medium heat. Add garlic, thyme and marjoram; cook and stir 1 to 2 minutes. Add quinoa; cook and stir 2 to 3 minutes. Stir in water; bring to a boil over high heat. Reduce heat to low; cover and simmer 15 to 20 minutes or until water is absorbed. (Quinoa will appear somewhat translucent.) Transfer quinoa to large bowl; gently stir in roasted vegetables.

Sweet Potato Shepherd's Pie

MAKES 6 SERVINGS

1 large sweet potato, peeled and cut into 1-inch pieces

1 large russet potato, peeled and cut into 1-inch pieces

¼ cup milk

¾ teaspoon salt

1 pound ground turkey

2 packages (4 ounces each) sliced mixed mushrooms *or* 8 ounces sliced cremini mushrooms

1 jar (12 ounces) beef gravy

½ teaspoon dried thyme

¼ teaspoon black pepper

¾ cup frozen baby peas, thawed

1. Combine sweet potato and russet potato in medium saucepan; add water to cover. Bring to a boil over medium-high heat. Reduce heat to low; cover and simmer 20 minutes or until potatoes are very tender. Drain potatoes; return to saucepan. Mash potatoes; stir in milk and salt. Preheat broiler.

2. Crumble turkey into large nonstick ovenproof skillet. Add mushrooms; cook and stir over medium-high heat until turkey is no longer pink and mushrooms begin to give off liquid. Drain.

3. Combine turkey mixture, gravy, thyme and pepper in same skillet; cook over medium heat 5 minutes. Add peas; cook and stir until heated through. Remove from heat; spread potato mixture over turkey mixture.

4. Broil 4 to 5 inches from heat source 5 minutes or until potatoes begin to brown.

Pork Chops with Bell Peppers and Sweet Potato

MAKES 4 SERVINGS

4 pork loin chops (4 ounces each), about ½ inch thick

1 teaspoon lemon-pepper seasoning

1 tablespoon olive oil

½ cup water

1 tablespoon lemon juice

1 teaspoon dried fines herbes, crushed

½ teaspoon beef bouillon granules

1¼ cups red or yellow bell pepper strips or a combination

1 cup sliced peeled sweet potato, cut into 1-inch pieces

¾ cup sliced onion

4 cups hot cooked rice

1. Rub both sides of pork chops with lemon-pepper seasoning. Heat oil in large skillet over medium-high heat. Add pork; cook 5 minutes or until browned on both sides.

2. Combine water, lemon juice, fines herbes and bouillon in small bowl; pour over pork. Reduce heat to medium-low; cover and cook 5 minutes.

3. Add bell pepper, sweet potato and onion to skillet; return to a boil. Reduce heat to low; cover and cook 10 to 15 minutes or until pork is barely pink in center and vegetables are crisp-tender. Remove pork and vegetables from skillet; keep warm.

4. Bring remaining juices in skillet to a boil over high heat. Reduce heat to medium; cook until sauce thickens slightly, stirring occasionally. Serve sauce with pork, vegetables and rice.

Bean and Vegetable Burritos

MAKES 4 SERVINGS

2   tablespoons chili powder

2   teaspoons dried oregano

1½ teaspoons ground cumin

1   large sweet potato, peeled and diced

1   can (about 15 ounces) black beans, rinsed and drained

4   cloves garlic, minced

1   medium onion, halved and thinly sliced

1   jalapeño pepper, seeded and minced*

1   green bell pepper, chopped

1   cup frozen corn, thawed and drained

3   tablespoons lime juice

1   tablespoon chopped fresh cilantro

¾   cup (3 ounces) shredded Monterey Jack cheese

4   (10-inch) flour tortillas

Lime wedges and salsa (optional)

Jalapeño peppers can sting and irritate the skin, so wear rubber gloves when handling peppers and do not touch your eyes.

Slow Cooker Directions

1. Combine chili powder, oregano and cumin in small bowl; mix well.

2. Layer ingredients in slow cooker in the following order: sweet potato, beans, half of chili powder mixture, garlic, onion, jalapeño, bell pepper, remaining half of chili powder mixture and corn.

3. Cover; cook on LOW 5 hours or until sweet potato is tender. Stir in lime juice and cilantro.

4. Preheat oven to 350°F. Spoon 2 tablespoons cheese in center of each tortilla. Top with 1 cup filling. Fold two sides over filling and roll up. Place burritos, seam side down, on baking sheet. Cover with foil and bake 20 to 30 minutes or until heated through. Serve with lime wedges and salsa, if desired.

Vegetarian Rice Noodles

MAKES 4 SERVINGS

½ cup soy sauce

⅓ cup sugar

¼ cup lime juice

2 fresh red Thai chiles *or* 1 large jalapeño pepper,* finely chopped

8 ounces thin rice noodles (rice vermicelli)

¼ cup vegetable oil

8 ounces firm tofu, drained and cut into triangles

1 jicama (8 ounces), peeled and chopped *or* 1 can (8 ounces) sliced water chestnuts, drained

2 medium sweet potatoes (1 pound), peeled and cut into ¼-inch-thick slices

2 large leeks, cut into ¼-inch slices

¼ cup chopped unsalted dry-roasted peanuts

2 tablespoons chopped fresh mint

2 tablespoons chopped fresh cilantro

*Chile peppers can sting and irritate the skin, so wear rubber gloves when handling peppers and do not touch your eyes.

1. Combine soy sauce, sugar, lime juice and chiles in small bowl; mix well. Set aside.

2. Place rice noodles in medium bowl. Cover with hot water; let stand 15 minutes or until soft. Drain well; cut into 3-inch lengths.

3. Meanwhile, heat oil in large skillet over medium-high heat. Add tofu; stir-fry 4 minutes per side or until golden. Remove with slotted spatula to paper towel-lined baking sheet.

4. Add jicama to skillet; stir-fry 5 minutes or until lightly browned. Remove to baking sheet. Stir-fry sweet potatoes in batches until tender and browned; remove to baking sheet. Add leeks; stir-fry 1 minute and remove to baking sheet.

5. Stir soy sauce mixture; add to skillet. Heat until sugar dissolves. Add noodles; toss to coat. Gently stir in tofu, vegetables, peanuts, mint and cilantro.

Side
Dishes

Skillet Roasted Root Vegetables

MAKES 4 SERVINGS

1 sweet potato, peeled, cut in half lengthwise then cut crosswise into ½-inch slices

1 large red onion, cut into 1-inch wedges

2 parsnips, cut diagonally into 1-inch slices

2 carrots, cut diagonally into 1-inch slices

1 turnip, peeled, cut in half and then cut into ½-inch slices

2½ tablespoons olive oil

1½ tablespoons honey

1½ tablespoons balsamic vinegar

1 teaspoon coarse salt

1 teaspoon dried thyme

¼ teaspoon ground red pepper

¼ teaspoon black pepper

1. Preheat oven to 400°F.

2. Combine all ingredients in large bowl; toss to coat. Spread vegetables in single layer in large cast iron skillet.

3. Roast 1 hour or until vegetables are tender, stirring once halfway through cooking time.

Sweet Potato Gratin
MAKES 6 TO 8 SERVINGS

3 pounds sweet potatoes (about 5 large)

½ cup (1 stick) butter, divided

¼ cup plus 2 tablespoons packed brown sugar, divided

2 eggs

⅔ cup orange juice

2 teaspoons ground cinnamon, divided

½ teaspoon salt

¼ teaspoon ground nutmeg

⅓ cup all-purpose flour

¼ cup old-fashioned oats

⅓ cup chopped pecans or walnuts

1. Preheat oven to 350°F.

2. Bake sweet potatoes 1 hour or until tender. Let stand 5 minutes or until cool enough to handle. Cut sweet potatoes lengthwise into halves; scrape pulp from skins into large bowl.

3. Beat sweet potato pulp, ¼ cup butter and 2 tablespoons brown sugar in large bowl with electric mixer at medium speed until butter is melted. Add eggs, orange juice, 1½ teaspoons cinnamon, salt and nutmeg; beat until smooth. Pour into 6 (6-ounce) individual baking dishes or 1½-quart casserole.

4. Combine flour, oats, remaining ¼ cup brown sugar and ½ teaspoon cinnamon in medium bowl; mix well. Cut in remaining ¼ cup butter with pastry blender or two knives until mixture resembles coarse crumbs. Stir in pecans. Sprinkle evenly over sweet potato mixture.

5. Bake 25 to 30 minutes or until heated through. For crispier topping, broil 5 inches from heat source 2 to 3 minutes or until golden brown.

Sweet Potato Fries

MAKES 2 SERVINGS

1 large sweet potato
  (about 12 ounces)

2 teaspoons olive oil

¼ teaspoon coarse salt

¼ teaspoon black pepper

¼ teaspoon ground red pepper

  Honey or maple syrup
  (optional)

1. Preheat oven to 425°F. Spray baking sheet with nonstick cooking spray.

2. Peel sweet potato; cut lengthwise into long spears. Toss with oil, salt, black pepper and red pepper on prepared baking sheet. Spread sweet potato spears in single layer not touching.

3. Bake 20 to 30 minutes or until lightly browned, turning halfway through baking time. Serve with honey, if desired.

Sweet Potato, Wild and White Rice Dressing

MAKES 8 SERVINGS

½ cup (1 stick) butter

2 cups chopped onions

1½ cups chopped celery

3 cloves garlic, finely chopped

½ teaspoon ground ginger

½ teaspoon ground sage

¼ teaspoon dried rosemary

¼ teaspoon ground cinnamon

2 sweet potatoes (12 ounces each), peeled, cooked and cut into ½-inch pieces

1 package (14 ounces) country-style stuffing mix

1½ cups cooked white rice

1 cup golden raisins

1 cup toasted pecans, coarsely chopped

1 cup cooked wild rice

¾ teaspoon salt

½ teaspoon black pepper

1 can (about 14 ounces) reduced-sodium chicken broth

1. Preheat oven to 350°F. Spray 13×9-inch baking dish with nonstick cooking spray.

2. Melt butter in large skillet over medium-high heat. Add onions, celery, garlic, ginger, sage, rosemary and cinnamon; cook and stir 6 to 8 minutes or until onions are tender. Transfer to large bowl.

3. Add sweet potatoes, stuffing mix, white rice, raisins, pecans, wild rice, salt and pepper to onion mixture; stir gently. Drizzle broth over stuffing mixture; toss gently to moisten. Transfer to prepared baking dish.

4. Cover and bake 30 minutes or until heated through. Uncover; bake 30 minutes or until top is browned.

tip Instead of packaged stuffing mix, you can make your own. Place 7 slices of bread directly on oven racks; bake in a 225°F oven for 1 hour. Cut into cubes. Makes about 4 cups.

Sweet and Savory
Sweet Potato Salad

MAKES 6 SERVINGS

---

4 cups chopped cooked peeled sweet potatoes (4 to 6)

¾ cup chopped green onions

½ cup chopped fresh parsley

½ cup dried cherries

¼ cup plus 2 tablespoons rice wine vinegar

2 tablespoons coarse ground mustard

1 tablespoon extra virgin olive oil

¾ teaspoon garlic powder

¼ teaspoon black pepper

⅛ teaspoon salt

1. Combine sweet potatoes, green onions, parsley and cherries in large bowl; mix well.

2. Whisk vinegar, mustard, oil, garlic powder, pepper and salt in small bowl until well blended. Pour over sweet potato mixture; toss gently to coat. Serve immediately or refrigerate until ready to serve.

Sweet Potato Soufflé

MAKES 8 SERVINGS

1¼ pounds sweet potatoes
(about 3 medium)

1 tablespoon butter

¾ cup whipping cream

1 teaspoon salt

¼ teaspoon white pepper

¼ teaspoon ground nutmeg

5 egg whites

1. Place sweet potatoes in medium saucepan; add water to cover. Bring to a boil over high heat. Reduce heat to medium-low; cover and cook 20 minutes or until fork-tender. Drain and cool to room temperature.

2. Preheat oven to 375°F. Generously butter 1½-quart soufflé dish.

3. Peel sweet potatoes; transfer to large bowl. Add cream, salt, pepper and nutmeg; beat until smooth.

4. Beat egg whites in medium bowl with electric mixer at medium-high speed until stiff peaks form. Gently fold egg whites into potato mixture until well blended. Pour into prepared soufflé dish. Place soufflé dish in 13×9-inch baking pan; add hot water to baking pan to depth of 1 inch.

5. Bake 1 hour and 10 minutes or until knife inserted into center comes out clean.

Roasted Sweet Potatoes
with Bacon and Onions
MAKES 4 TO 6 SERVINGS

3 thick slices applewood-smoked or peppered bacon, diced

2 pounds sweet potatoes, peeled and cut into 2-inch pieces

2 medium onions, cut into 8 wedges

1 teaspoon salt

1 teaspoon dried thyme

¼ teaspoon black pepper

1. Preheat oven to 375°F.

2. Cook bacon in large deep skillet until crisp. Drain on paper towel-lined plate. Add sweet potatoes and onions to drippings in skillet; stir until coated. Stir in salt, thyme and pepper.

3. Spread mixture in single layer in ungreased 15×10-inch jelly-roll pan or shallow roasting pan.

4. Bake 40 to 50 minutes or until vegetables are tender and golden brown. Transfer to serving bowl; sprinkle with bacon.

Jamaican Grilled Sweet Potatoes

MAKES 6 SERVINGS

2　large sweet potatoes
　　(about 1½ pounds)

3　tablespoons packed
　　brown sugar

3　tablespoons melted butter,
　　divided

1　teaspoon ground ginger

1　tablespoon chopped fresh
　　cilantro

2　teaspoons dark rum

1. Pierce sweet potatoes in several places with fork; place on paper towel in microwave. Microwave on HIGH 5 to 6 minutes or until crisp-tender, rotating one-fourth turn halfway through cooking time. Let stand 10 minutes. Cut sweet potatoes diagonally into ¾-inch slices.

2. Prepare grill for direct cooking. Combine brown sugar, 1 tablespoon butter and ginger in small bowl; mix well. Stir in cilantro and rum; set aside.

3. Lightly brush one side of each sweet potato slice with half of remaining melted butter.

4. Grill sweet potatoes, butter side down, on covered grill over medium heat 4 to 6 minutes or until grillmarked. Brush tops with remaining melted butter; turn and grill 3 to 5 minutes or until grillmarked. Transfer to platter; drizzle with rum mixture.

Toasted Coconut-Pecan Sweet Potato Casserole

MAKES 4 SERVINGS

2 cans (15 ounces each) sweet potatoes in heavy syrup, drained

½ cup (1 stick) butter, softened

¼ cup packed brown sugar

1 egg

½ teaspoon vanilla

⅛ teaspoon salt

½ cup chopped pecans

¼ cup flaked coconut

2 tablespoons golden raisins

1. Preheat oven to 325°F. Spray 8-inch square baking dish with nonstick cooking spray.

2. Combine sweet potatoes, butter, brown sugar, egg, vanilla and salt in food processor or blender; process until smooth. Spoon into prepared baking dish; sprinkle with pecans, coconut and raisins.

3. Bake 22 to 25 minutes or until heated through and coconut is lightly browned.

Sweet-Spiced Sweet Potatoes

MAKES 4 SERVINGS

2 pounds sweet potatoes, peeled and cut into ½-inch pieces

¼ cup packed dark brown sugar

1 teaspoon ground cinnamon

½ teaspoon ground nutmeg

⅛ teaspoon salt

2 tablespoons butter, cut into small pieces

1 teaspoon vanilla

Slow Cooker Directions

1. Combine sweet potatoes, brown sugar, cinnamon, nutmeg and salt in slow cooker; mix well.

2. Cover; cook on LOW 7 hours or on HIGH 4 hours. Add butter and vanilla; stir gently until blended.

Sweet
Treats

Steamed Southern Sweet Potato Custard

MAKES 4 SERVINGS

1 can (15 ounces) cut sweet potatoes, drained

1 can (12 ounces) evaporated milk, divided

½ cup packed brown sugar

2 eggs, lightly beaten

1 teaspoon ground cinnamon

½ teaspoon ground ginger

¼ teaspoon salt

Whipped cream

Ground nutmeg

Slow Cooker Directions

1. Combine sweet potatoes and ¼ cup evaporated milk in food processor or blender; process until smooth. Add remaining milk, brown sugar, eggs, cinnamon, ginger and salt; process until well blended. Pour into ungreased 1-quart soufflé dish; cover tightly with foil.

2. Crumple large sheet of foil (about 15×12 inches); place in bottom of slow cooker. Pour 2 cups water over foil. Make foil handles.* Transfer dish to slow cooker using foil handles.

3. Cover; cook on HIGH 2½ to 3 hours or until skewer inserted into center comes out clean.

4. Use foil handles to lift dish from slow cooker; remove to wire rack. Uncover; let stand 30 minutes. Garnish with whipped cream and nutmeg.

To make foil handles, tear off 3 (18×3-inch) strips of heavy-duty foil. Crisscross strips so they resemble spokes of a wheel. Place dish in center of strips. Pull foil strips up and over dish and place it in slow cooker. Leave foil strips in while dish cooks so you can easily remove dish when it is finished cooking.

Pecan-Crusted
Sweet Potato Cheesecake

MAKES 16 SERVINGS

Crust

5 tablespoons butter, melted

1 cup finely crushed gingersnap cookies (about 20 (2-inch) cookies)

½ cup chopped pecans, toasted*

1 tablespoon sugar

⅛ teaspoon salt

Filling

4 packages (8 ounces each) cream cheese, softened

1¼ cups sugar

3 eggs

1 can (15 ounces) sweet potatoes in syrup, drained

1 cup whipping cream

2 teaspoons vanilla

½ to 1 tablespoon pumpkin pie spice

Whipped cream and pecan halves (optional)

*To toast pecans, spread on baking sheet. Bake in preheated 350°F oven 6 to 8 minutes or until lightly browned, stirring frequently.

1. Preheat oven to 350°F. Lightly spray 10-inch springform pan with nonstick cooking spray. Wrap double layer of heavy-duty foil around outside of pan.

2. For crust, combine butter, cookies, chopped pecans, 1 tablespoon sugar and salt in food processor; pulse until coarse crumbs form. Press evenly into bottom (not side) of prepared pan. Bake 8 minutes; remove to wire rack to cool slightly.

3. For filling, combine cream cheese, 1¼ cups sugar, eggs, sweet potatoes, cream, vanilla and pumpkin pie spice in food processor or blender; process until smooth. Pour into crust. Place springform pan in larger baking pan. Add hot water to come one third of the way up side of springform pan.

4. Bake 1½ hours or until slightly puffed, softly set and top is golden brown. Remove to wire rack to cool completely. Cover and refrigerate overnight. Garnish with whipped cream and pecan halves.

Ginger Sweet Potato Cake

MAKES 18 SERVINGS

1 package (about 15 ounces) spice cake mix

1⅓ cups water

1 cup mashed cooked or canned sweet potatoes (see Tip)

3 eggs, lightly beaten

2 tablespoons canola oil

1 tablespoon grated fresh ginger

1 container (8 ounces) thawed frozen whipped topping

1. Preheat oven to 350°F. Spray 13×9-inch baking pan with nonstick cooking spray.

2. Combine cake mix, water, sweet potatoes, eggs, oil and ginger in large bowl; beat according to package directions. Pour batter into prepared baking pan.

3. Bake 30 minutes or until toothpick inserted into center comes out clean. Cool completely in pan on wire rack.

4. Frost with whipped topping. Cover and refrigerate until ready to serve.

 tip 1 can (15 ounces) sweet potatoes in syrup, drained, yields about 1 cup mashed sweet potatoes.

Sweet Potato Pecan Pie

MAKES 8 SERVINGS

1 unbaked deep-dish 9-inch pie crust

1½ cups pecan halves

½ cup light corn syrup

1 egg white

2 cups puréed cooked sweet potatoes (about 1½ pounds uncooked sweet potatoes)

⅓ cup packed brown sugar

1 teaspoon vanilla

½ teaspoon ground cinnamon

¼ teaspoon salt

Pinch *each* ground nutmeg and ground cloves

2 eggs, beaten

Whipped cream (optional)

1. Preheat oven to 400°F.

2. Prick holes in bottom of crust with fork. Bake 10 minutes or until lightly browned. Cool completely on wire rack. *Reduce oven temperature to 350°F.*

3. Combine pecans, corn syrup and egg white in small bowl; mix well. Whisk sweet potatoes, brown sugar, vanilla, cinnamon, salt, nutmeg and cloves in large bowl until well blended. Beat in eggs until blended. Spread sweet potato mixture in crust; top with pecan mixture.

4. Bake 45 minutes or until filling is puffed and topping is golden brown. Cool completely on wire rack. Top with whipped cream, if desired.

Sweet Potato Coconut Bars

MAKES 2 DOZEN BARS

30 vanilla wafers, crushed (see Tip)

1½ cups finely chopped walnuts, toasted,* divided

1 cup sweetened flaked coconut, divided

¼ cup (½ stick) butter, softened

2 cans (15 ounces each) sweet potatoes, well drained and mashed (2 cups)

2 eggs

1 teaspoon ground cinnamon

½ teaspoon ground ginger

¼ to ½ teaspoon ground cloves

¼ teaspoon salt

1 can (14 ounces) sweetened condensed milk

1 cup butterscotch chips

To toast walnuts, spread on baking sheet. Bake in preheated 350°F oven 8 to 10 minutes or until lightly browned, stirring frequently.

1. Preheat oven to 350°F.

2. For crust, combine vanilla wafers, 1 cup walnuts, ½ cup coconut and butter in medium bowl; mix well. (Mixture will be dry and crumbly.) Place two thirds of crumb mixture into bottom of 13×9-inch baking pan, pressing down lightly to form even layer.

3. For filling, beat mashed sweet potatoes, eggs, cinnamon, ginger, cloves and salt in large bowl with electric mixer at medium-low speed until blended. Gradually add condensed milk; beat until well blended. Spread filling evenly over crust; top with remaining crumb mixture, pressing lightly into sweet potato layer.

4. Bake 25 to 30 minutes or until knife inserted into center comes out clean. Sprinkle with butterscotch chips, remaining ½ cup walnuts and ½ cup coconut. Bake 2 minutes. Cool completely in pan on wire rack. Cover and refrigerate 2 hours before serving.

 tip Vanilla wafers can be crushed in a food processor or in a resealable food storage bag with a rolling pin or meat mallet.

Gingersnap Sweet Potato Fool

MAKES 6 SERVINGS

2 cups puréed cooked sweet potatoes *or* 1 can (15 ounces) sweet potato purée

¼ cup packed brown sugar

½ teaspoon ground cinnamon

¼ teaspoon ground ginger

1 cup whipping cream

3 tablespoons powdered sugar

12 gingersnap cookies, coarsely crushed

1. Combine sweet potatoes, brown sugar, cinnamon and ginger in medium bowl; mix well.

2. Beat cream in large bowl with electric mixer at high speed until thickened. Gradually add powdered sugar; beat until stiff peaks form.

3. Layer half of gingersnaps in 2-quart glass bowl; top with half of sweet potato mixture and half of whipped cream. Repeat layers. Refrigerate 1 hour before serving.

 tip Coarsely crushed cookies give this dessert a crunchy texture. If you prefer a smoother texture, crush the cookies finely instead.

Bourbon-Laced Sweet Potato Pie

MAKES 8 SERVINGS

1 pound sweet potatoes, peeled and cut into 1-inch pieces (about 2 medium)

2 tablespoons butter

¾ cup packed brown sugar

1 teaspoon ground cinnamon

¼ teaspoon salt

2 eggs

¾ cup whipping cream

¼ cup bourbon or whiskey

Pastry for 9-inch pie (or half of 15-ounce package refrigerated pie crusts)

Whipped cream (optional)

1. Preheat oven to 350°F. Place sweet potatoes in large saucepan; add water to cover. Bring to a boil over high heat. Reduce heat to low; simmer 20 minutes or until very tender. Drain well; transfer to large bowl.

2. Add butter; beat with electric mixer at medium speed until smooth. Add brown sugar, cinnamon and salt; beat until smooth. Add eggs, one at a time, beating well after each addition. Beat in cream and bourbon.

3. Line 9-inch pie plate with crust; flute edge. Pour sweet potato mixture into crust.

4. Bake 50 minutes or until knife inserted near center comes out clean. Remove to wire rack to cool least 1 hour before serving. Serve warm or at room temperature. Top with whipped cream, if desired.

 tip Pie can be cooled completely, covered and refrigerated up to 24 hours. Let stand at room temperature at least 30 minutes before serving.

Frosted Spiced Sweet Potato Cake

MAKES 24 SERVINGS

1½ pounds sweet potato (1 very large or 2 medium), cut in half lengthwise and crosswise

1½ cups all-purpose flour

1¼ cups granulated sugar

2 teaspoons baking powder

1 teaspoon ground cinnamon

½ teaspoon baking soda

½ teaspoon salt

¼ teaspoon ground allspice

¾ cup canola oil

2 eggs

½ cup chopped walnuts or pecans, plus additional for garnish

½ cup raisins

Cream Cheese Frosting (recipe follows)

1. Place sweet potato in large saucepan; add water to cover. Cover and cook over medium heat 30 minutes or until fork-tender, adding additional water during cooking, if necessary. Drain sweet potato; peel and mash when cool enough to handle. (You should have 2 cups.)

2. Preheat oven to 325°F. Spray 13×9-inch baking pan with nonstick cooking spray.

3. Combine flour, granulated sugar, baking powder, cinnamon, baking soda, salt and allspice in medium bowl. Beat sweet potatoes, oil and eggs in large bowl with electric mixer at low speed until blended. Add flour mixture; beat at medium speed 30 seconds or until well blended. Stir in ½ cup walnuts and raisins. Spoon batter into prepared pan.

4. Bake 35 minutes or until toothpick inserted into center comes out clean. Cool completely in pan on wire rack.

5. Prepare Cream Cheese Frosting. Spread frosting over cake; sprinkle with additional walnuts. Store cake, covered, in refrigerator.

Cream Cheese Frosting: Beat 1 package (8 ounces) softened cream cheese and ¼ cup (½ stick) softened butter in medium bowl with electric mixer at medium-high speed until light and fluffy. Gradually add 1½ cups sifted powdered sugar and ¼ teaspoon salt; beat until well blended. Stir in ¼ teaspoon vanilla.

Maple-Sweet Potato Mini Cheesecakes

MAKES 12 SERVINGS

1 package (8 ounces) cream cheese, softened

½ cup vanilla yogurt

1 can (15 ounces) sweet potatoes, drained and mashed (see Tip)

½ cup pure maple syrup

1 teaspoon vanilla

½ teaspoon ground cinnamon

¼ teaspoon ground cloves

1 egg

1 egg white

12 mini graham cracker crusts

12 pecan halves

1. Preheat oven to 350°F. Beat cream cheese in large bowl with electric mixer at medium speed until creamy. Add yogurt; beat until smooth. Add mashed sweet potatoes, maple syrup, vanilla, cinnamon and cloves; beat until well blended. Beat in egg and egg white until blended.

2. Spoon about ⅓ cup sweet potato mixture into each crust. Top with pecan half. Place filled crusts on large baking sheet.

3. Bake 30 to 35 minutes or until set and knife inserted into centers comes out clean. Cool on wire rack 1 hour. Refrigerate before serving.

tip Mashing sweet potatoes by hand produces pie filling with a somewhat coarse texture. For a smoother texture, process sweet potatoes in a food processor.

Variation For one larger cheesecake, pour the sweet potato mixture into a 9-inch graham cracker crust. Bake 40 to 45 minutes or until a knife inserted into the center comes out clean.

Sweet Potato Phyllo Wraps
MAKES 12 WRAPS

4 sheets frozen phyllo dough, thawed

Nonstick cooking spray

¾ cup mashed cooked sweet potato

¾ teaspoon vanilla

½ teaspoon ground cinnamon

4 tablespoons finely chopped pecans

1 tablespoon maple syrup

1. Preheat oven to 375°F. Line baking sheet with parchment paper.

2. Unroll phyllo dough, keeping sheets stacked. Cover with large sheet of waxed paper and damp kitchen towel. Remove 1 sheet at a time; place on work surface with short side facing you. Spray edges with cooking spray.

3. Combine sweet potato, vanilla and cinnamon in small bowl; mix well. Spread 3 tablespoons sweet potato mixture across short edge of phyllo dough; sprinkle with 1 tablespoon chopped pecans. Roll up phyllo and filling jelly-roll style. Cut into thirds; place on prepared baking sheet. Repeat with remaining phyllo sheets, sweet potato filling and pecans. Spray tops of wraps with cooking spray.

4. Bake 15 to 20 minutes or until golden brown. Drizzle with maple syrup.

Squash

RECIPES

Acorn
Squash

Barley and Pear-Stuffed Acorn Squash

MAKES 6 SERVINGS

3 small acorn squash

2 cups vegetable broth

¾ teaspoon salt, divided

1 cup uncooked quick-cooking barley

2 tablespoons butter

1 small onion, chopped

1 stalk celery, chopped

¼ teaspoon black pepper

1 large unpeeled ripe pear, diced

½ cup chopped hazelnuts, toasted*

¼ cup maple syrup

½ teaspoon ground cinnamon

To toast hazelnuts, spread on baking sheet. Bake at 350°F 7 to 10 minutes or until lightly browned, stirring occasionally.

1. Preheat oven to 350°F. Pierce each squash with knife in several places. Microwave on HIGH 8 to 10 minutes or until tender, turning once. Let stand 5 minutes.

2. Meanwhile, combine broth and ½ teaspoon salt in large saucepan; bring to a boil over high heat. Stir in barley. Reduce heat to low; cover and simmer 12 minutes or until tender. (Do not drain.)

3. Cut squash in half lengthwise; remove and discard seeds. Arrange squash halves, cut side up, in large baking dish.

4. Melt butter in large skillet over medium heat. Add onion, celery, remaining ¼ teaspoon salt and pepper; cook and stir 5 minutes. Add pear; cook 5 minutes. Add barley, hazelnuts, maple syrup and cinnamon; mix well. Spoon into squash halves; cover dish with foil.

5. Bake 15 to 20 minutes or until heated through.

Barley and Apple-Stuffed Acorn Squash: Substitute 1 apple for the pear and walnuts for the hazelnuts.

 *note* The squash can be stuffed ahead of time. Prepare as directed and bake at 350°F 25 to 30 minutes or until heated through.

Acorn Squash Soup with Chicken and Red Pepper Meatballs

MAKES 2 SERVINGS

1 small acorn squash (about 12 ounces)

8 ounces ground chicken or turkey

1 red bell pepper, seeded and finely chopped

1 egg

1 teaspoon dried parsley flakes

1 teaspoon ground coriander

½ teaspoon black pepper

¼ teaspoon ground cinnamon

Pinch ground red pepper

3 cups vegetable broth

1. Place squash in microwaveable dish; pierce squash in several places with sharp knife. Microwave on HIGH 8 to 10 minutes or until tender. Cool 10 minutes.

2. Meanwhile, combine chicken, bell pepper, egg, parsley flakes, coriander, black pepper, cinnamon and red pepper in large bowl, mix lightly. Shape mixture into 8 meatballs.

3. Place meatballs in microwavable dish; microwave on HIGH 5 minutes or until cooked through. Set aside to cool.

4. Cut squash in half; remove and discard seeds. Scrape squash pulp from shell into large saucepan; mash with potato masher. Add broth and meatballs to saucepan; cook over medium-high heat 12 minutes, stirring occasionally. Add additional liquid if necessary.

Curried Eggplant, Squash and Chickpea Stew

MAKES 2 SERVINGS

---

1 teaspoon olive oil

½ cup diced red bell pepper

¼ cup diced onion

1¼ teaspoons curry powder

1 clove garlic, minced

½ teaspoon salt

1¼ cups cubed peeled eggplant

¾ cup cubed peeled acorn or butternut squash

⅔ cup canned chickpeas, rinsed and drained

½ cup vegetable broth or water

3 tablespoons dry white wine

Hot pepper sauce (optional)

¼ cup lemon yogurt (optional)

2 tablespoons chopped fresh parsley (optional)

1. Heat oil in medium saucepan over medium heat. Add bell pepper and onion; cook and stir 5 minutes. Stir in curry powder, garlic and salt; cook and stir 1 minute.

2. Add eggplant, squash, chickpeas, broth and wine; bring to a boil. Reduce heat to low; cover and simmer 20 to 25 minutes or just until eggplant and squash are tender.

3. Season with hot pepper sauce, if desired. Serve with yogurt and parsley.

Harvest Casserole

MAKES 4 SERVINGS

1 pound bulk pork sausage

2 medium to large acorn squash (about 2 pounds each)

1 cup cooked rice

½ cup dried cranberries

½ teaspoon salt

½ teaspoon ground cinnamon

½ teaspoon black pepper

1 can (10¾ ounces) condensed chicken broth, divided

1. Preheat oven to 350°F. Spray 11×7-inch baking dish with nonstick cooking spray.

2. Heat large skillet over medium-high heat. Crumble sausage into skillet; cook and stir 5 minutes or until browned. Drain fat. Transfer sausage to large bowl.

3. Meanwhile, pierce squash in several places with sharp knife. Microwave on HIGH 8 minutes, turning once. When cool enough to handle, cut ½ inch off top and bottom of each squash and cut in half crosswise. Remove and discard seeds. Place squash halves in prepared baking dish.

4. Add rice, cranberries, salt, cinnamon and pepper to sausage; mix well. Stir in ¼ cup broth. Spoon sausage mixture into squash halves. Pour remaining broth into baking dish around squash.

5. Cover and bake 15 minutes. Uncover; bake 5 to 10 minutes or until squash is tender.

 tip For a side-dish casserole, eliminate the sausage and double the rice.

Glazed Maple Acorn Squash

MAKES 4 SERVINGS

1 large acorn or golden acorn squash

¼ cup water

2 tablespoons maple syrup

1 tablespoon butter, melted

¼ teaspoon ground cinnamon

1. Preheat oven to 375°F.

2. Cut tip and stem ends from squash; cut squash crosswise into 4 slices. Remove and discard seeds.

3. Pour water into 13×9-inch baking dish. Place squash in dish; cover with foil. Bake 30 minutes or until tender.

4. Combine maple syrup, butter and cinnamon in small bowl; mix well. Pour off water from baking dish. Brush squash with syrup mixture, letting excess pool in center of squash rings.

5. Bake, uncovered, 10 minutes or until syrup mixture is bubbly.

Indian Curry Stir-Fry

MAKES 4 SERVINGS

Cucumber-Mint Raita
(recipe follows)

2 small acorn squash (about
4 inches in diameter)

1 tablespoon vegetable oil

1 onion, thinly sliced

1 tablespoon minced fresh
ginger

1 red bell pepper, diced

1½ teaspoons curry powder

4 cloves garlic, minced

¾ pound boneless skinless
chicken thighs

2 tablespoons chopped
fresh cilantro

1. Prepare Cucumber-Mint Raita; refrigerate until ready to serve.

2. Cut squash in half lengthwise through stem ends; remove and discard seeds. Place squash halves, cut sides down, on microwavable plate; microwave on HIGH 10 to 12 minutes or until fork-tender. Cover and let stand 3 minutes or until cool enough to handle.

3. Heat oil in large skillet over high heat. Add onion and ginger; stir-fry 4 minutes or until onion is golden brown. Add bell pepper, curry powder and garlic; stir-fry 30 seconds or until fragrant. Add chicken; stir-fry 4 minutes or until chicken is cooked through. Remove from heat; stir in cilantro.

4. Spoon chicken mixture into squash halves. Serve with Cucumber-Mint Raita.

Cucumber-Mint Raita: Combine 1 cup plain yogurt, ½ cup diced cucumber and 2 tablespoons finely chopped fresh mint in medium bowl. Stir in 1 to 2 tablespoons lemon juice and 1 teaspoon honey, if desired; mix well.

Spicy Pork Stew
with Roasted Veggies

MAKES 8 SERVINGS

2 teaspoons olive oil, divided

1½ pounds boneless pork loin, trimmed and cut into ½-inch pieces

2 red bell peppers, cut into ½-inch pieces

1 package (8 ounces) sliced mushrooms

1 cup chopped onion

1 medium acorn squash, peeled and cut into ½-inch pieces

1 can (about 14 ounces) diced tomatoes

1 can (about 14 ounces) chicken broth

½ teaspoon salt

½ teaspoon red pepper flakes

½ teaspoon black pepper

½ teaspoon dried thyme

Fresh oregano sprigs (optional)

1. Heat 1 teaspoon oil in large saucepan or Dutch oven over medium-high heat. Add half of pork; cook about 5 minutes or until browned, stirring occasionally. Repeat with remaining oil and pork.

2. Add bell peppers, mushrooms and onion to saucepan; cook and stir 2 minutes.

3. Stir in squash, tomatoes, broth, salt, red pepper flakes, black pepper and thyme; bring to a boil over high heat. Reduce heat to low; cover and simmer 1 hour or until pork is tender. Garnish with oregano.

Couscous-Stuffed Squash

MAKES 4 SERVINGS

2 small acorn squash, halved lengthwise and seeded

1 medium poblano pepper, sliced

1 small onion, sliced

1¼ cups vegetable broth

½ cup shiitake mushrooms, chopped

¾ cup uncooked couscous

1 medium plum tomato, diced

2 tablespoons pine nuts

1. Preheat oven to 400°F. Spray baking sheet with nonstick cooking spray.

2. Place squash, cut side down, on prepared baking sheet. Spread pepper and onion on baking sheet. Cover with foil; bake 35 to 40 minutes or until squash is tender.

3. Combine broth and mushrooms in medium saucepan; bring to a boil over medium-high heat. Stir in couscous, tomato and pine nuts; remove from heat. Cover and let stand 5 minutes.

4. Meanwhile, dice roasted pepper and onion. Add to couscous mixture, fluffing couscous lightly with fork.

5. Turn squash cut side up; fill with couscous mixture.

 tip Acorn squash have thick, hard skins that can be difficult to cut. To make cutting easier, soften them in the microwave. Pierce the skin with a sharp knife or fork; microwave on HIGH 1 to 2 minutes. Let stand until cool enough to handle, then cut in half lengthwise and remove the seeds.

Butternut Squash

Balsamic Butternut Squash

MAKES 4 SERVINGS

3 tablespoons olive oil

2 tablespoons thinly sliced fresh sage (about 6 large leaves), divided

1 medium butternut squash, peeled and cut into 1-inch pieces (4 to 5 cups)

½ red onion, cut in half and cut into ¼-inch slices

1 teaspoon salt, divided

2½ tablespoons balsamic vinegar

¼ teaspoon black pepper

1. Heat oil in large cast iron skillet over medium-high heat. Add 1 tablespoon sage; cook and stir 3 minutes. Add butternut squash, onion and ½ teaspoon salt; cook 6 minutes, stirring occasionally. (Squash should fit into crowded single layer in skillet.) Reduce heat to medium; cook 15 minutes without stirring.

2. Add vinegar, remaining ½ teaspoon salt and pepper; cook 10 minutes or until squash is tender, stirring occasionally. Stir in remaining 1 tablespoon sage; cook 1 minute.

Butternut Squash-Apple Soup

MAKES 6 TO 8 SERVINGS

3 packages (12 ounces each) frozen cooked winter squash, thawed and drained

2 cans (about 14 ounces each) chicken broth

1 medium Golden Delicious apple, peeled and chopped

2 tablespoons minced onion

1 tablespoon packed brown sugar

1 teaspoon minced fresh sage or ½ teaspoon ground sage

¼ teaspoon ground ginger

½ cup whipping cream or half-and-half

Slow Cooker Directions

1. Combine squash, broth, apple, onion, brown sugar, sage and ginger in slow cooker.

2. Cover; cook on LOW 6 hours or on HIGH 3 hours.

3. Working in batches, blend soup in blender or food processor until smooth. Stir in cream just before serving.

 tip For thicker soup, use only 3 cups chicken broth.

Winter Squash Risotto

MAKES 4 TO 6 SERVINGS

2 tablespoons olive oil

1 small butternut squash or medium delicata squash, peeled and cut into 1-inch pieces (about 2 cups)

1 large shallot or small onion, finely chopped

½ teaspoon paprika

¼ teaspoon dried thyme

¼ teaspoon salt

¼ teaspoon black pepper

1 cup uncooked arborio rice

¼ cup dry white wine (optional)

4 to 5 cups hot reduced-sodium vegetable broth

½ cup shredded Parmesan or Romano cheese

1. Heat oil in large nonstick skillet over medium heat. Add squash; cook and stir 3 minutes. Add shallot; cook and stir 3 to 4 minutes or until squash is almost tender. Stir in paprika, thyme, salt and pepper. Add rice; stir to coat.

2. Add wine, if desired; cook and stir until wine is absorbed. Add broth, ½ cup at a time, stirring frequently until broth is absorbed before adding next ½ cup. Continue adding broth and stirring until rice is tender and mixture is creamy, 20 to 25 minutes.

3. Sprinkle with cheese just before serving.

Beef and Squash Slow Cooker Stew

MAKES 4 TO 6 SERVINGS

1 tablespoon vegetable oil

1 medium yellow onion, finely chopped

1 clove garlic, minced

2 cans (about 14 ounces each) diced tomatoes

2 cups 1-inch cubes butternut squash (about 1 small)

1 pound beef stew meat, cut into bite-size pieces

1 can (about 15 ounces) butter beans, rinsed and drained

½ cup beef broth

1 teaspoon minced jalapeño pepper*

½ teaspoon salt

½ teaspoon dried oregano

½ teaspoon chili powder

¼ teaspoon ground cumin

¼ teaspoon black pepper

*Jalapeño peppers can sting and irritate the skin, so wear rubber gloves when handling peppers and do not touch your eyes.

Slow Cooker Directions

1. Heat oil in medium skillet over medium heat. Add onion and garlic; cook and stir 5 to 8 minutes or until onion is golden brown. (Do not let garlic burn.) Transfer mixture to slow cooker.

2. Add tomatoes, squash, beef, beans, broth, jalapeño, salt, oregano, chili powder, cumin and black pepper to slow cooker.

3. Cover; cook on HIGH 5 to 7 hours. Turn off heat; let stew stand 30 minutes to thicken.

 tip To save time, skip step 1. Place the raw onion and garlic in the slow cooker. Add the remaining ingredients and proceed as directed above.

Turkey and Squash Tacos

MAKES 2 SERVINGS

4   crisp corn taco shells

2   teaspoons vegetable oil

¼   cup finely chopped onion

1   cup diced cooked butternut
    squash

1   teaspoon taco seasoning mix

1   cup chopped cooked turkey,
    warmed

Salt and black pepper

¼   cup salsa

1   avocado, peeled and cut
    into 8 thin wedges

1. Preheat oven to 325°F. Place taco shells on baking sheet; heat according to package directions.

2. Meanwhile, heat oil in large skillet over medium-high heat. Add onion; cook and stir 3 minutes. Add squash and taco seasoning mix; cook and stir 2 to 3 minutes.

3. Place ¼ cup turkey in each taco shell. Season with salt and pepper. Top with squash mixture, 1 tablespoon salsa and 2 slices avocado.

 Some supermarkets carry packaged diced squash; simply follow the cooking instructions on the package. To use a whole squash, peel the squash, cut in half and remove the seeds. Cut the squash into ¾-inch-long strips, then cut crosswise into ¾-inch chunks. Measure 1 cup squash. Heat 1 tablespoon vegetable oil in a medium skillet over medium-low heat. Add the squash; cook and stir 10 to 15 minutes or until fork-tender.

Spicy Squash and Chicken Soup

MAKES 4 SERVINGS

1 tablespoon vegetable oil

1 small onion, finely chopped

1 stalk celery, finely chopped

2 cups diced butternut squash
(about 1 small)

2 cups chicken broth

1 can (about 14 ounces) diced
tomatoes with chiles

1 cup chopped cooked chicken

½ teaspoon ground ginger

¼ teaspoon salt

⅛ teaspoon ground cumin

⅛ teaspoon black pepper

2 teaspoons lime juice

Fresh parsley or cilantro sprigs
(optional)

1. Heat oil in large saucepan over medium heat. Add onion and celery; cook and stir 5 minutes or just until vegetables are tender.

2. Stir in squash, broth, tomatoes, chicken, ginger, salt, cumin and pepper; bring to a boil. Reduce heat to low; cover and cook 30 minutes or until squash is tender. Stir in lime juice. Garnish with parsley.

Orange-Glazed Pork Chops with Butternut Squash and Cranberries

MAKES 4 SERVINGS

2 teaspoons olive oil

3 cups diced butternut squash

¼ cup orange juice

4 tablespoons orange marmalade, divided

¼ cup dried cranberries

4 boneless center-cut pork chops (about 4 ounces each), trimmed

½ teaspoon salt

¼ teaspoon black pepper

1. Heat oil in large nonstick skillet over medium heat. Add squash; cover and cook 15 minutes or until tender, stirring occasionally. Stir in orange juice, 2 tablespoons marmalade and cranberries; cook, uncovered, 1 minute or until almost all liquid evaporates.

2. Meanwhile, heat large heavy skillet over medium-high heat. Sprinkle pork with salt and pepper; cook 3 to 4 minutes per side or until barely pink in center.

3. Add remaining 2 tablespoons marmalade to skillet; cook over medium heat until melted, turning pork to coat with marmalade. Serve pork with squash mixture.

Lentil Chili

MAKES 5 SERVINGS

1 tablespoon canola oil

4 cloves garlic, minced

1 tablespoon chili powder

1 container (32 ounces) reduced-sodium vegetable broth

¾ cup dried brown or green lentils, rinsed and sorted

2 teaspoons chipotle hot pepper sauce

2 cups diced butternut squash

1 can (about 14 ounces) diced tomatoes

½ cup chopped fresh cilantro

¼ cup pepitas (pumpkin seeds) (optional)

1. Heat oil in large saucepan over medium heat. Add garlic; cook and stir 1 minute. Add chili powder; cook and stir 30 seconds.

2. Add broth, lentils and hot pepper sauce; bring to a boil over high heat. Reduce heat to low; simmer 15 minutes.

3. Stir in squash and tomatoes; simmer 18 to 20 minutes or until lentils and squash are tender. Top with cilantro and pepitas, if desired.

Ginger Squash Muffins

MAKES 12 MUFFINS

1½ cups all-purpose flour

⅓ cup whole wheat flour

⅓ cup granulated sugar

¼ cup packed dark brown sugar

2½ teaspoons baking powder

1 teaspoon ground cinnamon

½ teaspoon baking soda

½ teaspoon salt

½ teaspoon ground ginger

1 cup frozen winter squash, thawed*

2 eggs, beaten

⅓ cup canola oil

¼ cup finely chopped walnuts

2 tablespoons finely chopped crystallized ginger (optional)

One 12-ounce package frozen squash yields about 1 cup squash. Or, use 1 cup puréed cooked fresh butternut squash.

1. Preheat oven to 375°F. Spray 12 standard (2½-inch) muffin cups with nonstick cooking spray or line with paper baking cups.

2. Combine all-purpose flour, whole wheat flour, granulated sugar, brown sugar, baking powder, cinnamon, baking soda, salt and ground ginger in large bowl; mix well.

3. Whisk squash, eggs and oil in small bowl until well blended. Add to flour mixture; stir just until blended. *(Do not beat.)* Stir in walnuts and crystallized ginger, if desired. Spoon batter evenly into prepared muffin cups.

4. Bake 18 to 20 minutes or until toothpick inserted into centers comes out clean. Cool in pan 5 minutes; remove to wire rack to cool completely.

Honey-Roasted Chicken and Butternut Squash

MAKES 4 TO 6 SERVINGS

1 pound butternut squash, peeled and diced

Salt and black pepper

6 bone-in chicken thighs

1 tablespoon honey

1. Preheat oven to 375°F. Spray baking sheet and wire rack with nonstick cooking spray.

2. Spread squash on prepared baking sheet; season with salt and pepper.

3. Place wire rack over squash; place chicken on rack. Season with salt and pepper.

4. Roast 25 minutes. Carefully lift rack and stir squash. Brush honey over chicken. Roast 20 minutes or until chicken is cooked through (165°F).

Spaghetti Squash

Southwest Spaghetti Squash

MAKES 4 SERVINGS

1 spaghetti squash
   (about 3 pounds)

1 can (about 14 ounces)
   Mexican-style diced
   tomatoes

1 can (about 15 ounces) black
   beans, rinsed and drained

¾ cup (3 ounces) shredded
   Monterey Jack cheese,
   divided

¼ cup finely chopped
   fresh cilantro

1 teaspoon ground cumin

¼ teaspoon garlic salt

¼ teaspoon black pepper

1. Preheat oven to 350°F.

2. Spray baking sheet and 1½-quart baking dish with nonstick cooking spray. Cut squash in half lengthwise; remove and discard seeds. Place squash, cut side down, on prepared baking sheet.

3. Bake 45 minutes or just until tender. Separate squash into strands with fork; place in large bowl. (Use oven mitts to protect hands.) Add tomatoes, beans, ½ cup cheese, cilantro, cumin, garlic salt and pepper; mix well. Spoon into prepared baking dish; sprinkle with remaining ¼ cup cheese.

4. Bake 30 to 35 minutes or until heated through.

Spaghetti Squash Primavera

MAKES 4 SERVINGS

1 spaghetti squash
  (about 2 pounds)

1 tablespoon canola oil

½ teaspoon minced garlic

¼ cup finely chopped red onion

¼ cup thinly sliced carrot

¼ cup thinly sliced red
  bell pepper

¼ cup thinly sliced green
  bell pepper

1 can (about 14 ounces) Italian-
  style stewed tomatoes

½ cup thinly sliced yellow squash

½ cup thinly sliced zucchini

½ cup frozen corn, thawed

½ teaspoon dried oregano

⅛ teaspoon dried thyme

2 tablespoons grated Parmesan
  cheese

2 tablespoons finely chopped
  fresh parsley

1. Cut spaghetti squash in half lengthwise; remove and discard seeds. Place squash, cut side down, in large microwavable dish; cover with vented plastic wrap. Microwave on HIGH 9 minutes or until squash separates easily into strands when tested with fork.

2. Meanwhile, heat oil in large skillet over medium heat. Add garlic; cook and stir 1 minute. Add onion, carrot and bell peppers; cook and stir 3 minutes. Add tomatoes, yellow squash, zucchini, corn, oregano and thyme; bring to a boil. Reduce heat to low; cook 5 minutes or until vegetables are tender, stirring occasionally.

3. Separate squash into strands with fork. Spoon vegetable mixture over squash; top with cheese and parsley.

Spaghetti Squash Alfredo

MAKES 4 SERVINGS

4 cups cooked spaghetti squash (see Tip)

½ teaspoon salt

½ teaspoon black pepper

¼ cup (½ stick) butter

1 teaspoon minced garlic

1 cup whipping cream

½ cup grated Parmesan cheese, plus additional for garnish

1 tablespoon olive oil

12 ounces (about 2 cups) frozen cooked shrimp, thawed

Chopped fresh basil (optional)

1. Sprinkle squash with salt and pepper. Melt butter in large saucepan over medium-high heat. Add garlic; cook and stir 30 seconds. Add squash; cook and stir 2 to 3 minutes or until heated through.

2. Stir in cream; cook 3 minutes or until sauce begins to thicken. Stir in ½ cup cheese; cook 2 minutes or until cheese is melted. Cover and keep warm.

3. Meanwhile, heat oil in large nonstick skillet over high heat. Add shrimp; cook and stir until heated through.

4. Top squash mixture with shrimp; sprinkle with additional cheese and basil, if desired.

 Two medium spaghetti squash (3 to 4 pounds) will yield about 4 cups cooked squash. To cook squash quickly and easily, pierce each squash to the center with a knife in 2 places. Place the squash on a microwavable plate; microwave on HIGH 20 minutes. Let stand 10 minutes. Cut off the stem ends of the squash and cut them in half lengthwise. Remove and discard the seeds. Separate the squash into strands with a fork; drain in a colander.

Spaghetti Squash with Black Beans and Zucchini

MAKES 4 SERVINGS

1 spaghetti squash (about 2 pounds)

2 medium zucchini, cut lengthwise into ¼-inch-thick slices

2½ tablespoons extra virgin olive oil, divided

2 cups chopped seeded fresh tomatoes

1 can (about 15 ounces) black beans, rinsed and drained

2 tablespoons chopped fresh basil

2 tablespoons olive oil

2 tablespoons red wine vinegar

1 clove garlic, minced

½ teaspoon salt

1. Prepare grill for direct cooking. Pierce spaghetti squash in several places with fork. Place in center of large piece of heavy-duty foil. Bring two long sides of foil together above squash; fold down in series of locked folds, allowing room for heat circulation and expansion. Fold short ends up and over again. Press folds firmly to seal foil packet.

2. Grill squash, covered, over medium heat 45 minutes to 1 hour or until easily depressed with back of long-handled spoon, turning one quarter turn every 15 minutes. Remove squash from grill; let stand in foil 10 to 15 minutes.

3. Meanwhile, brush both sides of zucchini slices with ½ tablespoon oil. Grill, uncovered, over medium heat 4 minutes or until tender, turning once. Cut into bite-size pieces.

4. Remove spaghetti squash from foil. Cut squash in half lengthwise; remove and discard seeds. Separate squash into strands with fork; place on large serving plate.

5. Combine zucchini, tomatoes, beans and basil in medium bowl; mix well. Whisk remaining 2 tablespoons oil, vinegar, garlic and salt in small bowl until well blended. Add to vegetables; toss gently to coat. Serve vegetable mixture over spaghetti squash.

Turkey Meatballs
with Spaghetti Squash
MAKES 4 SERVINGS

⅓ cup soft whole wheat bread crumbs (1 slice bread)

¼ cup grated onion

1 teaspoon garlic powder

2½ tablespoons minced fresh Italian parsley

½ teaspoon red pepper flakes

1 teaspoon dried thyme

½ teaspoon whole fennel seeds

1 pound ground turkey

1 egg

1 small spaghetti squash (about 1 pound)

1 can (about 14 ounces) crushed tomatoes

¼ cup chicken broth

1 teaspoon dried oregano

1 tablespoon minced fresh basil

⅓ cup minced green onions

1. Combine bread crumbs, onion, garlic powder, parsley, red pepper flakes, thyme and fennel seeds in medium bowl; mix well. Combine turkey and egg in large bowl; add bread crumb mixture and knead until blended. Cover and refrigerate 10 minutes. Preheat broiler.

2. Cut squash in half lengthwise; remove and discard seeds. Place squash, cut side down, in glass baking dish; add 3 to 4 tablespoons water. Microwave on HIGH 10 to 12 minutes or until fork-tender. Set aside to cool.

3. Shape turkey mixture into 20 meatballs. Place meatballs in large baking pan. Broil meatballs 4 to 5 minutes; turn and broil 4 minutes.

4. Combine tomatoes and broth in large skillet; bring to a simmer over low heat. Add meatballs, oregano, basil and green onions; cook and stir about 10 minutes or until heated through.

5. Separate squash into strands with fork; top with meatballs and sauce.

Sesame Peanut Spaghetti Squash

MAKES 4 SERVINGS

1 spaghetti squash (3 pounds)

⅓ cup sesame seeds

⅓ cup vegetable broth

2 tablespoons reduced-sodium soy sauce

1 tablespoon sugar

2 teaspoons sesame oil

1 teaspoon cornstarch

1 teaspoon red pepper flakes

1 tablespoon vegetable oil

2 medium carrots, julienned

1 large red bell pepper, seeded and thinly sliced

¼ pound fresh snow peas, cut diagonally in half

½ cup coarsely chopped unsalted peanuts

⅓ cup minced fresh cilantro

1. Preheat oven to 350°F. Spray 13×9-inch baking dish with nonstick cooking spray. Cut squash in half lengthwise; remove and discard seeds. Place squash, cut side down, in prepared dish. Bake 45 minutes to 1 hour or until tender.

2. Separate squash into strands with fork. (Use oven mitts to hold hot squash.) Place squash in large bowl; cover and keep warm.

3. Heat large skillet over medium-high heat. Add sesame seeds; cook and stir 45 seconds or until golden brown. Transfer to blender. Add broth, soy sauce, sugar, sesame oil, cornstarch and red pepper flakes; blend until coarsely puréed.

4. Heat oil in large skillet over medium-high heat 1 minute. Add carrots; cook and stir 1 minute. Add bell pepper; cook and stir 2 minutes or until vegetables are crisp-tender. Add snow peas; cook and stir 1 minute. Stir sesame seed mixture; add to skillet. Cook and stir 1 minute or until sauce is thickened.

5. Serve sauce over spaghetti squash; top with peanuts and cilantro.

Neptune's Spaghetti Squash
MAKES 4 SERVINGS

1 spaghetti squash
(about 2 pounds)

3 tablespoons olive oil

1 clove garlic, minced

8 ounces medium raw shrimp,
peeled (with tails on)

8 ounces bay scallops

½ cup fresh or frozen peas

¼ cup sun-dried tomatoes in oil,
drained and chopped

½ teaspoon dried basil

¼ cup grated Parmesan cheese

1. Cut squash in half lengthwise; remove and discard seeds. Place squash, cut side down, in large microwavable dish; cover with vented plastic wrap. Microwave on HIGH 9 minutes or until squash separates easily into strands when tested with fork.

2. Meanwhile, heat oil in large skillet over medium-high heat. Add garlic; cook and stir 1 minute. Add shrimp, scallops, peas, tomatoes and basil; cook and stir 1 to 2 minutes or until shrimp are pink and opaque and scallops are opaque.

3. Separate squash into strands with fork. Top squash with seafood mixture; sprinkle with cheese.

Spicy Ratatouille
with Spaghetti Squash
MAKES 4 SERVINGS

1 spaghetti squash (2 pounds)

2 tablespoons olive oil

1 small onion, finely chopped

1 clove garlic, minced

1 small eggplant, trimmed and diced

1 small zucchini, trimmed and diced

1 cup coarsely chopped mushrooms, preferably oyster or shiitake

1 can (about 14 ounces) diced tomatoes

1 tablespoon canned chipotle peppers in adobo sauce, minced

½ teaspoon salt

½ teaspoon dried oregano

¼ teaspoon black pepper

Grated Parmesan cheese (optional)

1. Pierce squash several times with paring knife or fork. Place in microwavable dish; cover loosely with plastic wrap. Microwave on HIGH 12 to 13 minutes, turning once. (Squash is fully cooked when fork pierces skin and flesh easily.) Let stand 5 minutes or until cool enough to handle.

2. Cut squash in half lengthwise; remove and discard seeds. Separate squash into strands with fork. Measure 2 cups; cover and set aside. Save empty squash shell halves, if desired.*

3. Meanwhile, heat oil in large skillet over medium-high heat. Add onion and garlic; cook and stir 1 minute. Add eggplant, zucchini and mushrooms; cook and stir 5 minutes or until vegetables are lightly browned. Stir in tomatoes, chipotle peppers, salt, oregano and black pepper; cook over medium heat 3 to 5 minutes or until heated through and slightly thickened.

4. Place squash on serving platter; top with ratatouille. Sprinkle with cheese, if desired.

For a unique presentation, serve the ratatouille in the empty squash shell halves.

Yellow Squash

Middle Eastern Stuffed Squash

MAKES 4 SERVINGS

4 medium to large yellow squash

2 teaspoons olive oil, divided

12 ounces ground turkey

1 teaspoon ground cinnamon

½ cup finely chopped onion

1 ounce pine nuts, toasted*

¾ to 1 teaspoon sugar

½ teaspoon salt

¼ teaspoon ground cumin

⅛ teaspoon ground red pepper

½ cup plain yogurt

2 tablespoons chopped fresh mint

To toast pine nuts, spread in heavy skillet. Cook over medium heat 1 to 2 minutes or until nuts are lightly browned, stirring frequently.

1. Preheat oven to 350°F. Cut squash in half lengthwise. Scrape out pulp and seeds, leaving ½-inch shell. Chop pulp; set aside.

2. Heat 1 teaspoon oil in large skillet over medium-high heat. Add turkey and cinnamon; cook until no longer pink, stirring to break up meat. Transfer to plate.

3. Heat remaining 1 teaspoon oil in skillet over medium-high heat. Add onion and chopped squash; cook and stir 4 minutes or until squash is tender. Stir in turkey mixture, pine nuts, sugar, salt, cumin and red pepper until well blended.

4. Arrange squash halves, cut side up, in 13×9-inch baking pan. Spoon turkey mixture into squash halves. Cover with foil.

5. Bake 30 to 45 minutes or until squash is tender. Meanwhile, combine yogurt and mint in small bowl; mix well. Refrigerate until ready to serve. Serve squash with yogurt sauce.

Pasta Primavera
with Ricotta and Herbs

MAKES 4 SERVINGS

8 ounces uncooked fettuccine

1 cup ricotta cheese

½ cup milk

1 tablespoon olive oil

1 clove garlic, minced

½ teaspoon red pepper flakes

1½ cups sliced yellow squash

1½ cups sliced zucchini

1 cup red bell pepper strips

1 cup fresh or frozen peas

1 teaspoon Italian seasoning

¼ teaspoon salt

½ cup grated Parmesan cheese

1. Cook fettuccine according to package instructions; drain and keep warm. Whisk ricotta and milk in small bowl until well blended.

2. Heat oil in large skillet over medium heat. Add garlic and red pepper flakes; cook and stir 1 minute. Add yellow squash, zucchini, bell pepper, peas, Italian seasoning and salt; cook and stir 5 minutes or until vegetables are crisp-tender.

3. Combine fettuccine, vegetables and ricotta mixture in large bowl; toss to coat. Sprinkle with Parmesan.

Summer Squash Skillet

MAKES 4 SERVINGS

2 tablespoons butter

1 medium sweet or yellow onion, thinly sliced and separated into rings

2 medium yellow squash or zucchini or 1 of each, sliced

¾ teaspoon salt

¼ teaspoon black pepper

1 large tomato, chopped

¼ cup chopped fresh basil

2 tablespoons grated Parmesan cheese

1. Melt butter in large skillet over medium-high heat. Add onion; stir to coat with butter. Cover and cook 3 minutes. Reduce heat to medium; cook and stir about 3 minutes or until onion is golden brown.

2. Add squash, salt and pepper to skillet; cover and cook 5 minutes, stirring once. Add tomato; cook, uncovered, about 2 minutes or until squash is tender.

3. Stir in basil; sprinkle with cheese.

Sirloin Steak with Vegetable Salad

MAKES 4 SERVINGS

1 tablespoon olive oil

1 medium red bell pepper, quartered

1 medium yellow squash, halved lengthwise

1 medium onion, halved and separated

1 boneless beef top sirloin steak (about 1 pound)

1½ teaspoons steak seasoning

¼ teaspoon salt

½ cup grape tomatoes, halved

¼ cup vinaigrette dressing

2 ounces crumbled blue cheese

1. Heat oil in large skillet over medium-high heat. Add bell pepper; cook 2 to 3 minutes. Add squash and onion; cook 5 minutes per side or just until crisp-tender. Remove vegetables to cutting board.

2. Sprinkle both sides of steak with steak seasoning and salt. Add steak to skillet; cook over medium-high heat 4 minutes per side or to desired degree of doneness. Remove to cutting board; let stand 3 minutes before slicing.

3. Meanwhile, coarsely chop vegetables and place in medium bowl.

4. Add tomatoes and vinaigrette to vegetables; toss to coat. Add cheese; toss gently. Serve salad with steak.

Garden Potato Casserole

MAKES 5 SERVINGS

1¼   pounds unpeeled baking potatoes, thinly sliced

1   green or red bell pepper, thinly sliced

¼   cup finely chopped onion

2   tablespoons butter, cut into small pieces, divided

½   teaspoon dried thyme

Salt and black pepper

1   small yellow squash, thinly sliced

1   cup (4 ounces) shredded sharp Cheddar cheese

Slow Cooker Directions

1. Combine potatoes, bell pepper, onion, 1 tablespoon butter and thyme in slow cooker. Season with salt and black pepper; mix well. Layer squash over top; dot with remaining 1 tablespoon butter.

2. Cover; cook on LOW 7 hours or on HIGH 4 hours. Transfer potato mixture to serving bowl; sprinkle with cheese. Let stand 2 to 3 minutes or until cheese melts.

Spring Vegetable Ragoût

MAKES 6 SERVINGS

1 tablespoon olive oil

2 leeks, thinly sliced

3 cloves garlic, minced

1 package (10 ounces) frozen corn

1 cup vegetable broth

8 ounces yellow squash, halved lengthwise and cut into ½-inch pieces (about 1¼ cups)

6 ounces frozen shelled edamame

1 small package (4 ounces) shredded carrots

3 cups small cherry tomatoes, halved

1 teaspoon dried tarragon

1 teaspoon dried basil

1 teaspoon dried oregano

Salt and black pepper

Chopped fresh parsley (optional)

1. Heat oil in large skillet over medium heat. Add leeks and garlic; cook and stir just until fragrant. Add corn, broth, squash, edamame and carrots; cook and stir about 5 minutes or until squash is tender.

2. Stir in tomatoes, tarragon, basil and oregano. Reduce heat to low; cover and cook 2 minutes or until tomatoes are soft. Season with salt and pepper. Garnish with parsley.

Pepper and Squash Gratin

MAKES 6 SERVINGS

1 russet potato (12 ounces), unpeeled

8 ounces yellow summer squash, thinly sliced

8 ounces zucchini, thinly sliced

2 cups frozen bell pepper stir-fry blend, thawed

1 teaspoon dried oregano

½ teaspoon salt

⅛ teaspoon black pepper

½ cup grated Parmesan cheese or shredded sharp Cheddar cheese

1 tablespoon butter, cut into 8 pieces

1. Preheat oven to 375°F. Spray 12×8-inch glass baking dish with nonstick cooking spray.

2. Pierce potato several times with fork. Microwave on HIGH 3 minutes. Cut potato into thin slices.

3. Layer half of potato slices, yellow squash, zucchini, bell pepper blend, oregano, salt, black pepper and cheese in prepared baking dish. Repeat layers. Dot with butter; cover tightly with foil.

4. Bake 25 minutes or just until vegetables are tender. Uncover; bake 10 minutes or until lightly browned.

Vegetable Risotto
MAKES 4 TO 6 SERVINGS

2 tablespoons olive oil, divided

1 medium yellow squash, cubed

1 medium zucchini, cubed

1 cup chopped onion

1 cup sliced stemmed shiitake mushrooms

1 clove garlic, minced

3 plum tomatoes, seeded and chopped

1 teaspoon dried oregano

3 cups vegetable broth

1 cup uncooked arborio rice

¼ cup grated Parmesan cheese

Salt and black pepper

½ cup frozen peas, thawed

1. Heat 1 tablespoon oil in large saucepan over medium heat. Add yellow squash and zucchini; cook and stir 5 minutes or until crisp-tender. Transfer to medium bowl; set aside.

2. Add onion, mushrooms and garlic to saucepan; cook and stir 5 minutes or until tender. Add tomatoes and oregano; cook and stir 2 to 3 minutes or until tomatoes are softened. Transfer to bowl with zucchini mixture.

3. Heat broth in small saucepan over medium-low heat; keep warm.

4. Meanwhile, heat remaining 1 tablespoon oil in same saucepan over medium heat. Add rice; cook and stir 2 minutes.

5. Add broth, ¾ cup at a time, stirring frequently until broth is absorbed before adding next ¾ cup. Continue adding broth and stirring until rice is tender but still firm, 20 to 25 minutes.

6. Stir in cheese; season with salt and pepper. Stir in reserved vegetables and peas; cook until heated through. Serve immediately.

Bounty Soup

MAKES 4 SERVINGS

8 ounces yellow squash

1 tablespoon vegetable oil

12 ounces boneless skinless chicken breasts, cut into ½-inch pieces

2 cups frozen mixed vegetables

1 teaspoon dried parsley flakes

½ teaspoon salt

⅛ teaspoon dried rosemary

⅛ teaspoon dried thyme

⅛ teaspoon black pepper

1 can (about 14 ounces) chicken broth

1 can (about 14 ounces) stewed tomatoes

1. Cut wide part of squash in half lengthwise; lay flat and cut crosswise into ¼-inch-thick slices. Cut narrow part of squash into ¼-inch-thick slices.

2. Heat oil in large saucepan over medium-high heat. Add chicken; cook and stir 2 minutes. Add squash, mixed vegetables, parsley flakes, salt, rosemary, thyme and pepper; cook and stir 2 minutes.

3. Stir in broth and tomatoes, breaking large tomatoes apart; bring to a boil. Reduce heat to low; cover and cook 5 minutes or until vegetables are tender.

 tip Yellow squash, also known as summer squash, should be stored in the refrigerator and used within 5 days of purchase.

Summer Squash Bake

MAKES 8 SERVINGS

1 tablespoon vegetable oil

1 medium onion, cut into thin wedges

1 red bell pepper, cut into short thin strips

2 medium yellow squash, quartered and sliced (about 4 cups)

1 small zucchini, sliced (about 1½ cups)

½ teaspoon salt

¼ teaspoon black pepper

1 cup (4 ounces) shredded Cheddar cheese

1 cup soft bread crumbs (3 slices bread, crusts removed)

1½ tablespoons melted butter

½ teaspoon poultry seasoning

1. Preheat oven to 350°F.

2. Heat oil in large skillet over medium heat. Add onion and bell pepper; cook and stir 3 minutes. Add squash and zucchini, cook about 6 minutes or until vegetables are crisp-tender, stirring frequently. Stir in salt and pepper.

3. Transfer vegetable mixture to 1½- to 2-quart casserole; top with cheese. Combine bread crumbs, butter and poultry seasoning in small bowl; sprinkle over cheese.

4. Bake 30 to 35 minutes or until bread crumbs are browned.

Zucchini Squash

Zucchini-Tomato Frittata

MAKES 4 SERVINGS

1 tablespoon olive oil

1 cup sliced zucchini

1 cup broccoli florets

1 cup diced red or yellow
bell pepper

6 eggs, lightly beaten

½ cup cottage cheese

½ cup rehydrated sun-dried
tomatoes (1 ounce dry),
coarsely chopped*

¼ cup chopped green onions

¼ cup chopped fresh basil

⅛ teaspoon ground red pepper

2 tablespoons grated Parmesan
cheese

*To rehydrate sun-dried tomatoes, pour
1 cup boiling water over tomatoes in
small bowl; let stand 5 to 10 minutes or
until softened. Drain well before using.

1. Preheat broiler. Heat oil in 10-inch ovenproof skillet over high heat.
Add zucchini, broccoli and bell pepper; cook and stir 3 to 4 minutes
or until crisp-tender.

2. Whisk eggs, cottage cheese, sun-dried tomatoes, green onions, basil
and red pepper in medium bowl until well blended. Pour egg mixture
over vegetables in skillet. Cook, uncovered, gently lifting sides of
frittata so uncooked egg flows underneath. Cook 7 to 8 minutes or
until frittata is almost firm. Sprinkle with Parmesan.

3. Broil about 5 inches from heat 3 to 5 minutes or until golden brown.

Noodle-Free Lasagna

MAKES 8 SERVINGS

1 medium eggplant

2 medium zucchini

2 medium summer squash

1¼ pounds sweet Italian turkey sausage, casings removed

2 medium bell peppers, diced

2 cups mushrooms, thinly sliced

1 can (about 14 ounces) diced tomatoes

1 cup tomato sauce

½ cup coarsely chopped fresh basil

1 teaspoon dried oregano

½ teaspoon salt

¼ teaspoon black pepper

1 container (15 ounces) whole-milk ricotta cheese

2 cups (8 ounces) shredded mozzarella cheese

¼ cup grated Parmesan cheese

1. Cut eggplant, zucchini and yellow squash lengthwise into thin (⅛- to ¼-inch) slices. To reduce excess water, place slices in colander and drain 1 to 2 hours (see Tip).

2. Preheat oven to 375°F. Heat large nonstick skillet over medium-high heat. Add sausage; cook 8 to 10 minutes or until cooked through, stirring to break up meat. Drain fat. Transfer to plate.

3. Add bell peppers and mushrooms to skillet; cook and stir 3 to 4 minutes or until vegetables are tender. Return sausage to skillet. Add tomatoes, tomato sauce, basil, oregano, salt and black pepper; cook and stir 2 minutes or until heated through.

4. Layer one third of eggplant, zucchini and yellow squash in 13×9-inch nonstick baking pan. Spread half of ricotta over vegetables; top with one third of tomato sauce mixture. Sprinkle with half of mozzarella. Repeat layers once. Top with final layer of vegetables and tomato sauce mixture. Sprinkle with Parmesan; cover with foil.

5. Bake 45 minutes. Remove foil; bake 10 to 15 minutes or until vegetables are tender. Let stand 10 minutes before cutting.

 tip To reduce excess water from eggplant and squash, place the vegetable slices in a colander. Lay a paper towel or clean kitchen towel over the vegetables and weigh them down with a bowl or heavy cans. Let the vegetables drain for 1 to 2 hours before preparing the recipe. Or, bake the vegetables 10 minutes in a preheated 350°F oven to reduce the water content.

Crunchy Parmesan Zucchini Sticks
MAKES 6 APPETIZER SERVINGS

3 medium zucchini

1 package (3 ounces) ramen noodles, any flavor

½ cup shredded Parmesan cheese

½ cup all-purpose flour

1 egg

1 tablespoon water

Prepared marinara sauce

1. Preheat oven to 400°F. Line baking sheet with parchment paper.

2. Cut zucchini in half crosswise, then cut each half into 4 sticks.

3. Place noodles and cheese in food processor; pulse until fine crumbs form. Pour into shallow dish. Combine flour and seasoning packet from noodles in another shallow dish; mix well. Whisk egg and water in third shallow dish.

4. Working with one piece of zucchini at a time, dip zucchini first in flour, then egg, then noodle mixture, turning to coat. Place in single layer on prepared baking sheet.

5. Bake 20 minutes or until zucchini is softened and coating is golden brown. Serve warm with marinara sauce for dipping.

Buckwheat with Zucchini and Mushrooms

MAKES 4 TO 6 SERVINGS

1½ tablespoons olive oil

1 cup sliced mushrooms

1 medium zucchini, cut into ½-inch pieces

1 medium onion, chopped

1 clove garlic, minced

¾ cup buckwheat

½ teaspoon salt

¼ teaspoon dried thyme

⅛ teaspoon black pepper

1¼ cups vegetable broth

Lemon wedges (optional)

1. Heat oil in large nonstick skillet over medium heat. Add mushrooms, zucchini, onion and garlic; cook and stir 7 to 10 minutes or until vegetables are tender. Add buckwheat, salt, thyme and pepper; cook and stir 2 minutes.

2. Add broth; bring to a boil. Reduce heat to low; cover and cook 10 to 13 minutes or until liquid is absorbed and buckwheat is tender. Remove from heat; let stand, covered, 5 minutes. Serve with lemon wedges, if desired.

 tip For a meatier flavor, add pancetta to this dish. Coarsely chop 4 slices pancetta and cook in a large skillet over medium heat about 5 minutes to render the fat. Add 1 tablespoon olive oil, mushrooms, zucchini, onion and garlic to the skillet; proceed as directed above.

Zesty Vegetarian Chili

MAKES 4 SERVINGS

1 tablespoon canola or vegetable oil

1 large red bell pepper, coarsely chopped

2 medium zucchini or yellow squash (or 1 of each), cut into ½-inch pieces

4 cloves garlic, minced

1 can (about 14 ounces) fire-roasted diced tomatoes

¾ cup chunky salsa

2 teaspoons chili powder

1 teaspoon dried oregano

1 can (about 15 ounces) red kidney beans, rinsed and drained

10 ounces extra firm tofu, well drained and cut into ½-inch cubes

Chopped fresh cilantro (optional)

1. Heat oil in large saucepan over medium heat. Add bell pepper; cook and stir 4 minutes. Add zucchini and garlic; cook and stir 3 minutes.

2. Stir in tomatoes, salsa, chili powder and oregano; bring to a boil over high heat. Reduce heat to low; cook 15 minutes or until vegetables are tender.

3. Stir in beans; cook 2 minutes or until heated through. Stir in tofu; remove from heat. Garnish with cilantro.

Potato-Zucchini Pancakes

MAKES 6 PANCAKES (ABOUT 3 SERVINGS)

1 medium unpeeled baking potato, shredded

½ small zucchini, shredded

1 green onion, thinly sliced, plus additional for garnish

1 egg, lightly beaten

2 tablespoons all-purpose flour

Vegetable oil

Sour cream (optional)

1. Combine potato, zucchini, 1 green onion, egg and flour in medium bowl; mix well.

2. Heat ¼ inch oil in large heavy skillet over medium heat. Drop potato mixture by ⅓ cupfuls into skillet. Flatten pancakes with spatula; cook about 5 minutes per side or until browned.

3. Serve pancakes with sour cream; top with additional green onion, if desired.

Southwestern Chicken and Rice Skillet

MAKES 4 SERVINGS

1 teaspoon chili powder

1 teaspoon ground cumin

4 boneless skinless chicken breast halves (4 ounces each), pounded to ½-inch thickness

2 teaspoons canola oil

2 cloves garlic, minced

2 cups diced zucchini or yellow squash

½ cup salsa

1 package (8½ ounces) cooked brown rice

½ cup (2 ounces) shredded Mexican cheese blend

¼ cup chopped fresh cilantro

1. Combine chili powder and cumin; sprinkle over both sides of chicken.

2. Heat oil in large nonstick skillet over medium-high heat. Add chicken; cook 3 to 4 minutes per side or until chicken is no longer pink in center. Transfer to plate.

3. Add garlic to same skillet; cook 15 to 30 seconds. Add zucchini; cook and stir 3 minutes. Stir in salsa; cook 2 minutes or until zucchini is crisp-tender. Stir in rice; cook until heated through.

4. Return cooked chicken to skillet; top with cheese and cilantro. Cover and cook about 2 minutes until chicken is heated through and cheese is melted.

Herbed Zucchini Ribbons
MAKES 4 SIDE-DISH SERVINGS

3 small zucchini (about 12 ounces)

2 tablespoons olive oil

1 tablespoon white wine vinegar

2 teaspoons chopped fresh basil leaves *or* ½ teaspoon dried basil

½ teaspoon red pepper flakes

¼ teaspoon ground coriander

Salt and black pepper

1. Cut tip and stem ends from zucchini with paring knife. Using vegetable peeler, begin at stem end and make continuous ribbons down length of each zucchini.

2. Place steamer basket in large saucepan; add 1 inch of water. (Water should not touch bottom of basket.) Place zucchini ribbons in steamer basket; cover and bring to a boil over high heat. When pan begins to steam, check zucchini for doneness. (It should be crisp-tender.) Transfer zucchini to warm serving dish with slotted spatula or tongs.

3. Whisk oil, vinegar, basil, red pepper flakes and coriander in small bowl until well blended.

4. Pour dressing over zucchini; toss gently to coat. Season with salt and black pepper. Serve immediately or refrigerate up to 2 days.

Italian Pasta Soup with Fennel

MAKES 6 SERVINGS

---

1 tablespoon olive oil

1 small fennel bulb, trimmed and chopped into ¼-inch pieces (1½ cups)

4 cloves garlic, minced

3 cups vegetable broth

1 cup uncooked small shell pasta

1 medium zucchini or yellow summer squash, cut into ½-inch pieces

1 can (about 14 ounces) Italian-style diced tomatoes

¼ cup grated Romano or Parmesan cheese

¼ cup chopped fresh basil

Dash black pepper (optional)

1. Heat oil in large saucepan over medium heat. Add fennel; cook and stir 5 minutes. Add garlic; cook and stir 30 seconds. Add broth and pasta; bring to a boil over high heat. Reduce heat to low; simmer 5 minutes.

2. Stir in zucchini; simmer 5 to 7 minutes or until pasta and vegetables are tender.

3. Stir in tomatoes; cook until heated through. Top with cheese, basil and pepper, if desired.

Butterscotch Malt Zucchini Cake

MAKES 10 TO 12 SERVINGS

2½ cups all-purpose flour

4 tablespoons malted milk powder

1 teaspoon baking soda

½ teaspoon baking powder

½ teaspoon salt

½ teaspoon ground nutmeg

1¾ cups packed brown sugar

½ cup (1 stick) butter, softened

½ cup vegetable oil

2 eggs

½ cup buttermilk

1 teaspoon vanilla

2 cups grated zucchini

¾ cup white chocolate chips, divided

¾ cup butterscotch chips, divided

½ cup chopped nuts

1. Preheat oven to 350°F. Grease and flour 12-cup (10-inch) bundt pan.

2. Combine flour, malted milk powder, baking soda, baking powder, salt and nutmeg in medium bowl; mix well.

3. Beat brown sugar, butter, oil and eggs in large bowl with electric mixer at medium speed 2 minutes. Add buttermilk and vanilla; beat until well blended. Add flour mixture; beat at low speed just until blended. Stir in zucchini, ½ cup white chips, ½ cup butterscotch chips and nuts. Pour batter into prepared pan.

4. Bake 60 to 65 minutes or until toothpick inserted near center comes out clean. Cool in pan 10 minutes; invert onto wire rack to cool completely.

5. Place remaining ¼ cup white chips in small microwavable bowl; microwave on HIGH 30 seconds. Stir; microwave in 10-second intervals, if necessary, until melted and smooth. Drizzle over cake. Repeat with remaining ¼ cup butterscotch chips. Let stand until set.

METRIC CONVERSION CHART

VOLUME MEASUREMENTS (dry)

1/8 teaspoon = 0.5 mL
1/4 teaspoon = 1 mL
1/2 teaspoon = 2 mL
3/4 teaspoon = 4 mL
1 teaspoon = 5 mL
1 tablespoon = 15 mL
2 tablespoons = 30 mL
1/4 cup = 60 mL
1/3 cup = 75 mL
1/2 cup = 125 mL
2/3 cup = 150 mL
3/4 cup = 175 mL
1 cup = 250 mL
2 cups = 1 pint = 500 mL
3 cups = 750 mL
4 cups = 1 quart = 1 L

VOLUME MEASUREMENTS (fluid)

1 fluid ounce (2 tablespoons) = 30 mL
4 fluid ounces (1/2 cup) = 125 mL
8 fluid ounces (1 cup) = 250 mL
12 fluid ounces (1 1/2 cups) = 375 mL
16 fluid ounces (2 cups) = 500 mL

WEIGHTS (mass)

1/2 ounce = 15 g
1 ounce = 30 g
3 ounces = 90 g
4 ounces = 120 g
8 ounces = 225 g
10 ounces = 285 g
12 ounces = 360 g
16 ounces = 1 pound = 450 g

DIMENSIONS

1/16 inch = 2 mm
1/8 inch = 3 mm
1/4 inch = 6 mm
1/2 inch = 1.5 cm
3/4 inch = 2 cm
1 inch = 2.5 cm

OVEN TEMPERATURES

250°F = 120°C
275°F = 140°C
300°F = 150°C
325°F = 160°C
350°F = 180°C
375°F = 190°C
400°F = 200°C
425°F = 220°C
450°F = 230°C

BAKING PAN SIZES

Utensil	Size in Inches/Quarts	Metric Volume	Size in Centimeters
Baking or	8×8×2	2 L	20×20×5
Cake Pan	9×9×2	2.5 L	23×23×5
(square or	12×8×2	3 L	30×20×5
rectangular)	13×9×2	3.5 L	33×23×5
Loaf Pan	8×4×3	1.5 L	20×10×7
	9×5×3	2 L	23×13×7
Round Layer	8×1½	1.2 L	20×4
Cake Pan	9×1½	1.5 L	23×4
Pie Plate	8×1¼	750 mL	20×3
	9×1¼	1 L	23×3
Baking Dish	1 quart	1 L	—
or Casserole	1½ quart	1.5 L	—
	2 quart	2 L	—